Quick & Easy
Kids' Cakes

Quick & Easy Kids' Cakes

50 GREAT CAKES FOR CHILDREN OF ALL AGES

SARA LEWIS

Bounty Books

First published in Great Britain in 2006 by Hamlyn
a division of Octopus Publishing Group Ltd

This edition published in 2009 by Bounty Books,
a division of Octopus Publishing Group Ltd
Endeavour House,189 Shaftesbury Avenue,London WC2H 8JY
www.octopusbooks.co.uk

Reprinted 2010

An Hachette UK Company
www.hachette.co.uk

ISBN: 978-0-753718-92-6

A CIP catalogue record for this book is available from the
British Library

Printed and bound in China

Dedication

For Nicky and her powers of peruasion.

Notes

Standard level spoon measurements are used in all recipies.

1 tablespoon = one 15 ml spoon

1 teaspoon = one 5 ml spoon

Medium eggs should be used unless otherwise stated.

Both metric and imperial measurements have been given. Use one set
of measurements only, and not a mixture of both.

Ovens should be preheated to the specified temperature - if using a
fan-assisted oven, follow the manufacturers instructions for adjusting
the time and temperature.

Contents

Introduction

For young children or the young at heart, nothing beats the thrill of blowing out the candles on your birthday cake, but as a busy working parent, the idea of finding the time to make a cake that is extra special can fill you with horror.

Over the next few pages, you will find 50 quick and easy cakes to delight tiny tots and melt the heart of even the coolest older child. Some can be decorated in 20 minutes or so, while others will take around an hour. The cakes may be baked and frozen in advance to spread the workload, and most can be made with equipment that you will already have in your kitchen cupboards. Alternatively, cheat and buy a plain cake from your local supermarket. All cakes can be made by even the most inexperienced of cake makers – you may just find that it takes you a few minutes longer to do. Don't be put off if you have never made a cake before. If you can roll out frozen pastry, you can roll out and cover a cake with ready-to-roll icing. Very often it is the simplest cake that is the most eye-catching.

In the first section of the book, you will find all the basic recipes for making the cakes themselves, with tips on flavour variations, recipes for different icings and fillings, plus advice and techniques on achieving that special finish. The main section features cake designs for both younger and older children, boys and girls, decorated with butter icing, ready-to-roll icing, chocolate and sweets. There is something for everyone, from a cute pastel-coloured tortoise to an inviting white chocolate puppy; from jewelled pink crowns or mini birthday cakes to a sweet-guzzling monster, a grown-up game of chess and a scary ghostly face.

But you don't have to wait for a birthday to try these cakes. They make great school raffle prizes or can simply be made with the children as a fun way to cheer up a dreary day in the school holidays. Whatever the occasion, making and decorating your own cake is a great way to show just how much you care.

Equipment

The recipes in this book are generally quick and easy to make and assemble, so the amount of equipment you will need is minimal. You will probably find that you already have most of the items of equipment you need, with perhaps the exception of some of the more specialist tiny icing cutters. If you are new to cake making, it is worth checking which tins are required before you begin baking so that you are not disappointed.

If there is a piece of equipment you need to buy, it's well worth visiting your local cake-decorating shop. They are usually packed with cutters, tools, ready-made decorations, coloured icings and almost every shade of food colouring imaginable. However, if you don't have a convenient local shop, you will find that many of the larger kitchenware companies offer a comprehensive mail-order service.

BASIC EQUIPMENT

- kitchen scales
- baking tins
- greaseproof paper and nonstick baking paper
- paper cake cases
- scissors
- pastry brush
- artists' paintbrushes
- selection of bowls in various sizes
- large and small sieve – a new tea strainer is ideal
- large serrated knife for cutting cakes in half, round-bladed knife for spreading butter icing, large and small cook's knives for cutting icing shapes
- large and small palette knives
- large and small rolling pins
- whisk
- biscuit cutters and selection of small/mini cutters

Tip

If you like cooking, the chances are that you will already have most of the equipment that you need, with the exception of specialist cutters or cake boards.

CAKE TINS

Most cake tins can be found in the cookware department of your local large department store or hardware shop or large supermarket. For more unusual equipment, visit a specialist cookware or cake-decorating shop, or check out appropriate websites on the Internet. If buying new tins, opt for the better-quality ranges, as they will last for 20 years or more without denting or warping. A loose-bottomed tin makes it easier to remove a cake, but is not essential. Likewise, flexible muffin and fairy cake moulds are easy to use, but rigid metal ones work just as well.

MOST FREQUENTLY USED CAKE TINS

- 23 cm (9 inch) deep round tin
- 20 cm (8 inch) deep square tin
- 2 x 20 cm (8 inch) straight-sided sandwich tins
- 18 cm (7 inch) deep round tin
- 12-section bun tray
- 30 x 23 x 5 cm (12 x 9 x 2 inch) roasting tin

Lining a deep round tin

Brush the sides and base of the tin lightly with a little oil, then cut strips of greaseproof paper a little taller than the side of the tin. Fold a strip about 1 cm (½ inch) in from one long edge, then snip up to the fold line at intervals. Stand the paper in the tin so that the cut edges sit flat on the base of the tin. Cut and add extra paper strips, overlapping the ends of the strips slightly, as necessary to cover the entire side of the tin. Using the tin as a guide, stand it on some more greaseproof paper, draw around the tin, then cut out the round and press on to the base of the tin. Brush the paper lightly with more oil. If using nonstick baking paper instead of greaseproof paper, simply add the paper shapes to the dry tin.

Lining a deep square tin

Cut strips of paper a little taller than the sides of the tin, just as when lining a round tin, but snip up to the fold line only where the paper is pressed into the corners of the tin. Cut a square of paper for the base in just the same way as for a round tin.

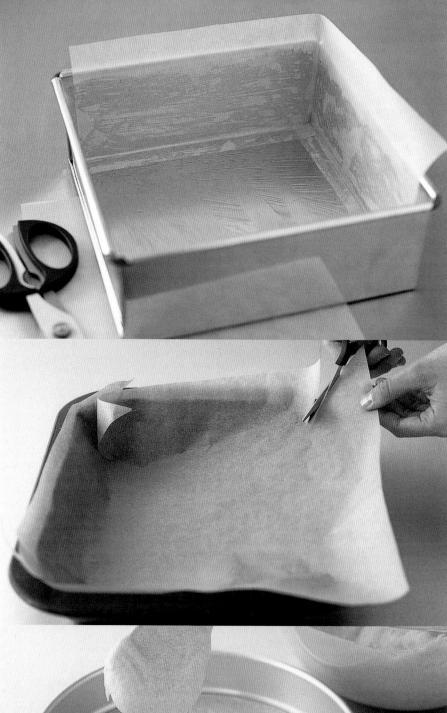

Lining a roasting tin

Cut a piece of nonstick baking paper a little larger than the tin, then make diagonal cuts into the corners. Press the paper into the tin, tucking the snipped edges one behind the other so that the base and sides of the tin are completely lined in one action. You can use greaseproof paper instead of nonstick baking paper, but you will need to grease both the tin and the paper.

Lining a sandwich tin

Brush the base and side of the tin with a little oil, then stand the tin on top of a piece of greaseproof paper, draw around the tin and cut out the round of paper. Lay over the base of the tin and brush lightly with a little extra oil.

Cake recipes

Most of the cakes in this book are based on two simple cake mixes: a Madeira cake and a quick-mix sandwich cake. These mixtures are then baked in a variety of different items of bakeware – you'll be surprised to find just how many shapes can be conjured up from a few cake tins, pudding basins, the odd mixing bowl and a roasting tin. Make and bake the cake the day before the party or freeze it a week or so in advance, un-iced. This section also includes recipes for individual cakes – fairy cakes and muffins – plus a Swiss roll. For people short of time, shop-bought equivalents have been listed, where available, on main recipes.

MADEIRA CAKES

This traditional creamed cake is made by beating butter or soft margarine with sugar until light and fluffy. Gradually mix in beaten eggs and self-raising flour until smooth. Alternating eggs and flour will prevent the eggs curdling or separating the mixture. Unlike an all-in-one cake, this has a greater proportion of flour to fat and sugar and produces a light, slightly closer-textured cake that can be cut and shaped well, making it ideal for that special birthday cake.

Small Madeira Cake

175 g (6 oz) soft margarine or butter, at room temperature

175 g (6 oz) caster sugar

3 eggs

1 tablespoon milk

225 g (7½ oz) self-raising flour

FLAVOURINGS

Vanilla **1 teaspoon vanilla extract**

Lemon **grated rind of ¾ lemon; replace milk with 1 tablespoon lemon juice**

Orange **grated rind of ¾ orange; replace milk with 1 tablespoon orange juice**

Chocolate **replace 50 g (2 oz) flour with same weight of cocoa powder**

The above amount will fill:

SIZE OF CONTAINER	BAKING TIME
18 cm (7 inch) deep round cake tin	45–50 minutes
15 cm (6 inch) deep square cake tin	45–50 minutes
20 cm (8 inch) mixing bowl	50–60 minutes
1.2 litre (2 pint) pudding basin	1 hour 10 minutes

Medium Madeira Cake

250 g (8 oz) soft margarine or butter, at room temperature

250 g (8 oz) caster sugar

4 eggs

2 tablespoons milk

300 g (10 oz) self-raising flour

1 teaspoon baking powder (for roasting tin cake only)

FLAVOURINGS

Vanilla **2 teaspoons vanilla extract**

Lemon **grated rind of 1 lemon; replace milk with 2 tablespoons lemon juice**

Orange **grated rind of 1 orange; replace milk with 2 tablespoons orange juice**

Chocolate **replace 65 g (2½ oz) flour with same weight of cocoa powder**

The above amount will fill:

SIZE OF CONTAINER	BAKING TIME
30 x 23 x 5 cm (12 x 9 x 2 inch) roasting tin	30–35 minutes
1.5 litre (2½ pint) pudding basin	1¼ –1½ hours
2 x 900 ml (1½ pint) pudding basins	about 1 hour
1.2 litre (2 pint) and 750 ml (1¼ pint) pudding basins	1 hour 5 minutes – 1hour 10 minutes for larger basin cake, 55–60 minutes for smaller basin cake
20 cm (8 inch) single sandwich tin cake and 900 ml (1½ pint) pudding basin	30 minutes for sandwich cake, about 1 hour for basin cake

Large Madeira Cake

375 g (12 oz) soft margarine or butter, at room temperature

375 g (12 oz) caster sugar

6 eggs

4 tablespoons milk

625 g (1¼ lb) self-raising flour

FLAVOURINGS

Vanilla **3 teaspoons vanilla extract**

Lemon **grated rind of 2 lemons; replace milk with 4 tablespoons lemon juice**

Orange **grated rind of 2 oranges; replace milk with 4 tablespoons orange juice**

Chocolate **replace 100 g (3½ oz) flour with same weight of cocoa powder**

The above amount will fill:

SIZE OF CONTAINER	BAKING TIME
23 cm (9 inch) deep round cake tin	1–1¼ hours
20 cm (8 inch) deep square cake tin	1–1¼ hours

 Cream the margarine or butter and sugar together in a bowl until light and fluffy. Beat the eggs and milk, or eggs only if you are making a fruit-flavoured cake, in a small bowl with a fork. Mix the flour with the cocoa powder and baking powder, if using, in a separate small bowl. Add alternate spoonfuls of the egg mixture and flour and beat into the creamed mixture until they have all been incorporated and the cake mixture is smooth. Beat in the vanilla extract or grated lemon or orange rind and juice, if using.

2 Spoon the cake mixture into your chosen greased and lined tin. Bake in a preheated oven, 160°C (325°F), Gas Mark 3, for the appropriate time (see boxed text), until well risen and golden brown and a skewer comes out of the centre of the cake cleanly (see page 19). Leave for 10 minutes in the tin, then loosen the edges with a palette knife, turn out on to a wire rack and leave to cool completely.

QUICK-MIX CAKES

This is a quick and easy all-in-one cake that can be made in minutes and may be used for varying-sized sandwich cakes and fairy cakes. Quite simply, all the ingredients are put into the bowl at the same time and beaten for just a few minutes until smooth and creamy. If you are using butter, the secret is to have it at room temperature so that it will beat easily either with a wooden spoon, electric mixer or food processor. As the mixing time is so brief, a little baking powder is added to boost the raising agent in the self-raising flour and to guarantee success every time.

Large round Quick-mix Sandwich Cake

250 g (8 oz) soft margarine

250 g (8 oz) caster sugar

250 g (8 oz) self-raising flour

1 teaspoon baking powder

4 eggs

FLAVOURINGS

Vanilla **1 teaspoon vanilla extract**

Lemon **grated rind of 1 lemon**

Orange **grated rind of 1 small orange**

Chocolate **replace 40 g (1½ oz) flour with same weight of cocoa powder**

1 Put all the ingredients into a bowl, with your chosen flavouring, if using, and beat together until smooth.

2 Spoon the cake mixture into 2 x 20 cm (8 inch) greased and base-lined sandwich tins (see page 11).

3 Bake in a preheated oven, 180°C (350°F), Gas Mark 4, for about 25 minutes until springy to the touch (see page 19). Leave for 5 minutes in the tins, then turn out on to a wire rack and leave to cool completely.

Medium round Quick-mix Sandwich Cake

175 g (6 oz) soft margarine

175 g (6 oz) caster sugar

175 g (6 oz) self-raising flour

½ teaspoon baking powder

3 eggs

FLAVOURINGS

Vanilla **¾ teaspoon vanilla extract**

Lemon **grated rind of ¾ lemon**

Orange **grated rind of ¾ small orange**

Chocolate **replace 25 g (1 oz) flour with same weight of cocoa powder**

1 Put all the ingredients into a bowl, with your chosen flavouring, if using, and beat together until smooth.

2 Spoon the cake mixture into 2 x 18 cm (7 inch) greased and base-lined sandwich tins (see page 11).

3 Bake in a preheated oven, 180°C (350°F), Gas Mark 4, for about 20 minutes until springy to the touch (see page 19). Leave for 5 minutes in the tins, then turn out on to a wire rack and leave to cool completely.

Small round Quick-mix Sandwich Cake

125 g (4 oz) soft margarine

125 g (4 oz) caster sugar

125 g (4 oz) self-raising flour

¼ teaspoon baking powder

2 eggs

FLAVOURINGS

Vanilla ½ teaspoon vanilla extract

Lemon grated rind of ½ lemon

Orange grated rind of ½ small orange

Chocolate replace 2 tablespoons flour with the same weight of cocoa powder

1 Put all the ingredients into a bowl, with your chosen flavouring, if using, and beat together until smooth.

2 Spoon the cake mixture into 2 x 15 cm (6 inch) greased and base-lined sandwich tins (see page 11).

3 Bake in a preheated oven, 180°C (350°F), Gas Mark 4, for about 15 minutes until springy to the touch (see page 19). Leave for 5 minutes in the tins, then turn out on to a wire rack and leave to cool completely.

Tip

Some sandwich tins have slightly sloping sides. These are fine to use if the cake is just sandwiched together and topped with icing, but if you plan to cover the sides of the cake with icing, you will need straight-sided tins, otherwise the finished cake will have an unsatisfactory appearance.

Fairy Cakes

Makes 12

125 g (4 oz) soft margarine

125 g (4 oz) caster sugar

125 g (4 oz) self-raising flour

2 eggs

FLAVOURINGS

Vanilla ½ **teaspoon vanilla extract**

Lemon **grated rind of ½ lemon**

Orange **grated rind of ½ small orange**

Chocolate **replace 2 tablespoons flour with same weight of cocoa powder**

1 Line a 12-section bun tray with paper cake cases. Put all the ingredients into a bowl, with your chosen flavouring, if using, and beat together until smooth.

2 Divide the cake mixture evenly between the paper cake cases using a dessertspoon and level the surface.

3 Bake in a preheated oven, 180°C (350°F), Gas Mark 4, for 15 minutes until springy to the touch (see page 19). Leave for 5 minutes in the tray, then remove cakes to a wire rack and leave to cool completely.

Shallow Cake

50 g (2 oz) soft margarine

50 g (2 oz) caster sugar

50 g (2 oz) self-raising flour

⅛ teaspoon baking powder

1 egg

1 Put all the ingredients into a bowl and beat together with a wooden spoon or an electric mixer until smooth.

2 Spoon into an 18 cm (7 inch) greased and base-lined sandwich tin (see page 11).

3 Bake in a preheated oven, 180°C (350°F), Gas Mark 4, for 12–15 minutes until springy to the touch (see page 19). Leave for 5 minutes in the tin, then turn out on to a wire rack and leave to cool completely.

MUFFINS
Makes 12

300 g (10 oz) plain flour

3 teaspoons baking powder

125 g (4 oz) light muscovado sugar

3 eggs

4 tablespoons sunflower oil

50 g (2 oz) butter, melted

150 g (5 oz) natural yogurt

FLAVOURINGS

Vanilla **2 teaspoons vanilla extract**

Chocolate **replace 40 g (1½ oz) flour with same weight of cocoa powder**

Double chocolate **replace 40 g (1½ oz) flour with same weight of cocoa powder and add 100 g (3½ oz) diced milk chocolate**

1 Line a 12-section deep muffin tray with paper cake cases. Put all the ingredients into a bowl, with your chosen flavouring, if using, and combine with a fork until only just mixed.

2 Divide the muffin mixture evenly between the paper cases using a dessertspoon.

3 Bake the muffins in a preheated oven, 190°C (375°F), Gas Mark 5, for 18–20 minutes until they are well risen and the tops are golden brown and have cracked slightly. Leave for 5 minutes in the tray, then remove cakes to a wire rack and leave to cool completely.

SWISS ROLL

Makes one 28 cm (11 inch) long Swiss roll

4 large eggs

125 g (4 oz) caster sugar, plus extra for sprinkling

125 g (4 oz) plain flour

1 tablespoon hot water

8 tablespoons raspberry or strawberry jam

FLAVOURING

Chocolate **replace 25 g (1 oz) flour with the same weight of cocoa powder and use chocolate spread in place of jam**

1 Line a 37 x 28 cm (15 x 11 inch) roasting tin with nonstick baking paper (see page 11), so that the paper stands about 2.5 cm (1 inch) high all around the sides. Put the eggs and sugar in a large heatproof bowl set over a saucepan of simmering water and whisk, ideally using a hand-held electric whisk, for about 10 minutes until very thick and pale and the mixture leaves a trail when the whisk is lifted just above the bowl.

2 Sift in the flour and use a large metal spoon to fold it into the egg mixture, adding the measured water once most of the flour is incorporated.

3 Turn the cake mixture into the tin and ease gently into the corners. Bake in a preheated oven, 200°C (400°F), Gas Mark 6, for 10–12 minutes until pale golden and just firm to the touch.

4 While the cake is baking, wet a clean tea towel with hot water, wring it out and put on the work surface so that the short edges are facing you. Cover with a sheet of greaseproof paper and sprinkle evenly with sugar.

5 Turn the cake out on to the paper and peel off the lining paper. Spread the cake with the jam, then roll up, starting from the short edge nearest to you. Put the Swiss roll, seam side down, on to a wire rack to cool.

IS MY CAKE COOKED?

If your cake looks well risen and brown but you are not sure if it is ready, there are several methods of checking it. Insert a skewer into the centre of a deep cake. If it comes out cleanly, it is ready, but if there is a smearing of cake mixture, put the cake back in the oven and test again at five- or ten-minute intervals, depending on how messy the skewer is.

For sandwich cakes and fairy cakes, press the top of the cake lightly with a fingertip. If the cake springs back, then it is ready. If the finger mark remains, then return the cake to the oven and test again in five minutes' time.

All ovens vary slightly, so use the timings as a guide and check shortly before the end of the baking time to see how your cake or cakes are doing. Resist the temptation to keep opening the oven, especially midway through cooking, or your cake will sink. If you have a fan-assisted oven, adjust the temperature slightly and reduce by 10°C (25°F), because these ovens can run hot. For larger cakes, check two-thirds of the way through the baking time and cover the top loosely with foil if the cake is browning too quickly.

SLICING THE TOP OFF A CAKE

With the exception of sandwich cakes, most cakes tend to peak during cooking and will need trimming before icing. The deeper the cake, the more it will rise in the centre. Trim the top level using a large serrated knife and then turn large cakes upside down before icing. Trim the tops of fairy cakes if spooning over glacé icing so that it will form a flat even layer and not run off the cake.

SHORT OF TIME?

Cheat and buy a cake from the supermarket. With lots of flavoured muffins, fairy cakes, Swiss rolls and filled sandwich cakes to choose from, it can be a lifesaver for a busy working mum. Look out for thick slices of plain or marbled Madeira cake and sandwich three or four side by side to make a larger square cake. Larger bought round sponge cakes may be more difficult to find, so buy whatever size you can and just scale the design down and make a slightly smaller version.

icings and fillings

Some icings – including butter icing and ganache – are used as both a filling for a cake and as a delicious coating. Others, such as ready-to-roll icing, are used only as a cake covering. Refer to the individual recipes for guidance.

READY-TO-ROLL ICING

For speed, most of us will opt to buy this icing from the supermarket, but if you would prefer to make your own, it really is very easy. If you can't find liquid glucose – it is usually sold alongside the vanilla extract and other flavourings in supermarkets – then order it from your local chemist. Don't be tempted to leave it out, as it is crucial to the icing's elasticity. You will also find small boxes of dried egg white with the other baking ingredients in the supermarket, and, because it is pasteurized, it does not pose any potential health risk as in the case of raw egg white.

Makes 500 g (1 lb)

1 dried egg white

2 tablespoons liquid glucose

500 g (1 lb) icing sugar, sifted

1 Reconstitute the egg white with water according to the packet instructions.

2 Put the egg white into a large bowl with the liquid glucose, then gradually work in the sugar with a wooden spoon, kneading it with your hands straight on to the work surface when too stiff to stir. The mixture should be smooth and elastic, and you may find that you do not need to mix in all the sugar.

Tip

Ready-to-roll icing dries out quickly, so make sure that it is tightly wrapped in a plastic bag until you are ready to use it.

BUTTER ICING

Sometimes known as buttercream, this is a soft spreading icing that can be used plain or flavoured, spread smooth or roughed up or even coloured to fill and decorate cakes. For the best flavour, use good-quality unsalted butter at room temperature, or soften in the microwave, so that it is easy to mix with the icing sugar. A newly opened pack of icing sugar may be used straight from the pack, but if you have a pack that has been open a while, you may need to sift it before using to remove any lumps. Follow the method below and refer to the table for ingredient quantities and optional flavourings.

1 Put the butter into a bowl and soften with a wooden spoon or beat in a food processor.

2 Gradually beat in the sugar, then add the milk and/or your chosen flavouring, and mix to a soft spreading consistency.

QUANTITY	Single	One and a half	Double
unsalted butter, at room temperature	50 g (2 oz)	75 g (3 oz)	125 g (4 oz)
icing sugar	125 g (4 oz)	175 g (6 oz)	250 g (8 oz)
milk	1 teaspoon	2 teaspoons	1 tablespoon
FLAVOURINGS			
Vanilla	½ teaspoon vanilla extract	¾ teaspoon vanilla extract	1 teaspoon vanilla extract
Lemon	1 teaspoon grated lemon rind and 1 teaspoon lemon juice in place of milk	1½ teaspoons grated lemon rind and 2 teaspoons lemon juice in place of milk	2 teaspoons grated lemon rind and 1 tablespoon lemon juice in place of milk
Orange	1 teaspoon grated orange rind and 1 teaspoon orange juice in place of milk	1½ teaspoons grated orange rind and 2 teaspoons orange juice in place of milk	2 teaspoons grated orange rind and 1 tablespoon orange juice in place of milk
Chocolate	4 teaspoons cocoa powder dissolved in 2 teaspoons boiling water in place of milk	2 tablespoons cocoa powder dissolved in 4 teaspoons boiling water in place of milk	8 teaspoons cocoa powder dissolved in 2 tablespoons boiling water in place of milk

CHOCOLATE FUDGE ICING

This dark icing thickens as it cools, so if you get delayed and the icing has set too much to spread, beat in a little boiling water. This quantity will cover an 18 cm (7 inch) deep round or 15 cm (6 inch) deep square Small Madeira Cake (see page 12).

25 g (1 oz) butter

15 g (½ oz) cocoa powder

175 g (6 oz) icing sugar (no need to sift)

2 tablespoons milk

pinch of ground cinnamon (optional)

1 Melt the butter in a small saucepan over a low heat. Stir in the cocoa powder and cook over a medium heat, stirring constantly, for 30 seconds until smooth.

2 Remove from the heat and gradually stir in the sugar and milk, mixing until smooth. Mix in the ground cinnamon, if using.

3 Return to the heat and cook for 1 minute, stirring constantly, until the icing has a glossy pouring consistency. Quickly spread over the cake while the icing is still warm.

GLOSSY CHOCOLATE BUTTER ICING

A rich, dark, shiny icing made with a mixture of plain dark and milk chocolate so that it is full of flavour but without the bitterness of plain dark chocolate that children dislike. This quantity will cover a 23 cm (9 inch) deep round or 20 cm (8 inch) deep square Medium Madeira Cake (see page 13).

50 g (2 oz) butter

100 g (3½ oz) good-quality milk chocolate

100 g (3½ oz) good-quality plain dark chocolate

50 g (2 oz) icing sugar (no need to sift)

2 tablespoons milk

1 Melt the butter in a small saucepan over a low heat. Break the chocolate into pieces, add to the pan and heat gently, stirring occasionally, until just melted.

2 Remove from the heat and stir in the sugar and the milk. Return to the heat, if necessary, stirring constantly, until the icing is smooth and glossy. Use immediately.

Tip

As an alternative, this icing could be flavoured with a little finely grated orange rind or instant coffee powder.

DOUBLE CHOCOLATE GANACHE

A rich creamy icing made with warmed cream and half plain dark and half milk chocolate. It will set as it cools, so make it about 1 hour before you need it. This amount will cover an 18 cm (7 inch) deep round or 15 cm (6 inch) deep square Small Madeira Cake (see page 12). For a larger quantity, use 300 ml (½ pint) double cream and 300 g (10 oz) chocolate.

200 ml (7 fl oz) double cream

100 g (3½ oz) good-quality milk chocolate

100 g (3½ oz) good-quality plain dark chocolate

1 Heat the cream in a small saucepan over a medium heat until it is almost boiling and just beginning to bubble around the edges.

2 Remove the pan from the heat, break the chocolate into pieces and add to the pan. Set aside for 10 minutes or so, stirring occasionally, until the chocolate has melted.

3 Cover with clingfilm, leave to cool then chill in the refrigerator for 30 minutes–1 hour until thickened enough to hold its shape. The time will vary depending on how hot the cream was.

Tip

If you get delayed and the icing chills for longer – soften it once more by standing the basin in a saucepan of just boiled water for a minute or two. Stir before using.

WHITE CHOCOLATE CREAM

Deliciously chocolaty, this cream can be used to fill and cover an 18 cm (7 inch) deep round vanilla- or chocolate-flavoured Small Madeira Cake (see page 12) or a 23 cm (9 inch) deep round Medium Madeira Cake (see page 13), cut into 8 individual cakes using a 6 cm (2½ inch) plain biscuit cutter or upturned tumbler as a template using a small serrated knife, as for the White Chocolate Treats on page 93.

150 g (5 oz) white chocolate

300 ml (½ pint) double cream

1 Break the chocolate into pieces and put in a heatproof bowl set over a half-filled saucepan of just-boiled water. Set aside for 5 minutes, off the heat, until the chocolate has melted.

2 Whip the cream in a large bowl until it forms soft swirls. Stir the melted chocolate, then gently fold into the cream. Use immediately.

GLACÉ ICING

A quick-to-make, spoonable icing that can be used plain or coloured. If your child has adventurous tastes, try replacing the water with orange or lemon juice. This quantity will cover 12 Fairy Cakes (see page 16).

175 g (6 oz) icing sugar, sifted

3–4 teaspoons water

1 Sift the sugar into a medium bowl, pressing the last grains through the sieve with the back of a spoon.

2 Gradually stir in just enough of the measurement water to mix to a smooth thick icing that will flow from a spoon.

ROYAL ICING

Most often used to decorate wedding and Christmas cakes, here royal icing is also used to pipe on cake details or to stick icing decorations in place. Royal icing sets hard as it dries, so if making it in advance, cover the surface closely with clingfilm, stir before using and loosen the mixture with a few drops of lemon juice, if necessary.

1 dried egg white

225 g (7½ oz) icing sugar, sifted

1. Reconstitute the egg white with water according to the packet instructions.

2. Gradually whisk in the sugar a tablespoon or so at a time until the icing forms soft peaks that hold their shape. You may find that you do not need to add all the sugar.

Tip

Dried egg white is generally sold in small sachets that are the equivalent to two egg whites – make sure that you use only half a packet.

Techniques

The individual cake designs in this book detail the specific
techniques involved in icing and decorating the cakes,
but the following are the basic techniques that are routinely used.

USING READY-TO-ROLL ICING

Ready-to-roll icing may be sold plain white, in ivory or in a variety
of pastel and vibrant colours ranging from pale lilac, pink and blue
to cerise pink, turquoise, orange or purple and the deepest red
or black. Whether you choose to buy white and colour your own
with food colourings (see below) or buy ready coloured, the icing
should be kneaded on a surface lightly dusted with a little sifted
icing sugar to soften it slightly before rolling. Any icing that you are
not going to use immediately must be tightly wrapped in a plastic
bag or clingfilm so that it does not dry out.

FOOD COLOURINGS

These can be used to colour ready-to-roll icing, royal icing and
butter icing, as well as desiccated coconut. They are most often
sold in paste or liquid form and are very concentrated, so add
them cautiously. For very intense, deep colours, opt for paste
colourings. Reserve liquid colourings for creating pastel shades
of icing, as the more of these you add, the stickier your icing can
become, especially when using ready-to-roll icing. Add dots of
colouring from the tip of a cocktail stick and gradually build up
the colour until you achieve the desired shade, kneading well
between additions. You can always add a little extra, but once
added, the only way to reduce the colour is to mix with more
icing. Sometimes a marbled effect is required. In this case, only
partially mix in the colouring, then roll out for a colour-veined finish.

CHOOSING A CAKE BOARD

Traditionally, birthday cakes were always served on thick or thin foil-covered cake boards, but now with such a wide choice of coloured chinaware and other items and materials on offer, you may prefer to serve your cake on a china plate, a coloured wood, glass or a plastic chopping board.

COVERING A CAKE BOARD
WITH READY-TO-ROLL ICING

1 Spread a little butter icing or jam thinly along the edge or edges of the cake board top.

2 Knead the ready-to-roll icing on a surface lightly dusted with sifted icing sugar until slightly softened. Lightly dust a rolling pin with icing sugar, then roll out the icing to a round or square a little larger (about 1 cm/½ inch) all around than the board, moving the icing and redusting the work surface lightly with icing sugar as needed.

3 Lift the icing on the rolling pin and drape it over the board. Smooth in place with your fingertips dusted with icing sugar.

4 Lift the board and trim off the excess icing around the edge or edges with a small knife.

5 Re-knead the icing trimmings, tightly wrap in a plastic bag or clingfilm and reserve.

Tip

For larger cake boards, you may find it easier to roll the icing straight on to the cake board lightly dusted with icing sugar with a rolling pin.

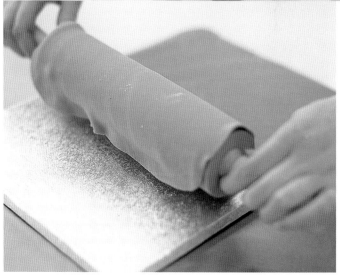

COVERING A CAKE WITH READY-TO-ROLL ICING

1 Put the cake on the cake board or plate and spread the top and side or sides thinly with butter icing or apricot jam.

2 Knead the ready-to-roll icing on a surface lightly dusted with sifted icing sugar. Lightly dust a rolling pin with icing sugar, then roll out the icing to a round or square about 12 cm (5 inches) larger in diameter than the cake top. Lift the icing on the rolling pin and drape over the cake.

3 Ease the icing over the sides of the cake, smoothing it with your fingertips dusted with icing sugar. As the icing is so pliable, you should be able to shape it without any creases.

4 Trim away the excess icing from the base of the board or plate with a small knife. Using the palms of your hands dusted with icing sugar, smooth out any bumps, making the surface as flat as you can.

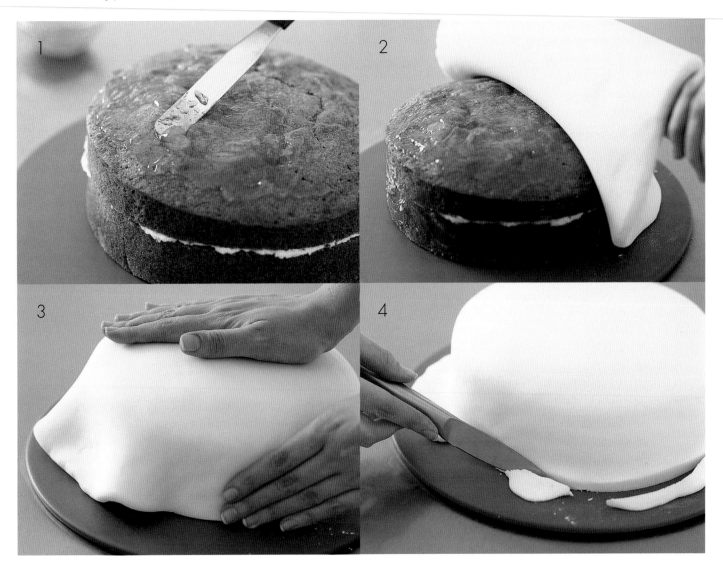

DECORATING A CAKE BOARD WITH AN ICING BORDER

Instead of covering a cake board with icing, you can add a border of icing to the cake board edge or edges once the cake has been decorated. Cut one long strip of rolled-out icing and join at the back of a round cake or cut strips the same length as the board sides of a square board and trim the ends diagonally so that the edges can be butted together neatly.

COVERING A CAKE WITH BUTTER ICING

1 Put the sandwiched cake on to a cake board or plate, then spread a little butter icing very thinly over the top and side or sides of the cake to stick the crumbs in place.

2 Spread a more generous layer of butter icing over the top and side or sides of the cake, smoothing in place with a small palette knife.

Finishing touches

This is the fun, creative part! But do not be nervous if you are a novice at cake icing. There are lots of inventive ways of using basic cut-out icing shapes, sweets and chocolates to add novelty and decorative details to your cakes with the minimum of time.

PIPED ICING

Tubes of ready-made icing with small detachable plastic piping tubes are sold in most supermarkets, as are smaller tubes of writing icing, which are ideal when only tiny amounts of piping are needed. Where larger amounts are required, you may prefer to use homemade royal icing (see page 25) and spoon it into a greaseproof paper piping bag. These are easy to make and you can simply snip off the tip to pipe the icing or use a piping tube.

CUTTING OUT ICING SHAPES

Stamping out shapes with cutters is a quick and easy way for even the most inexperienced at cake icing to decorate a cake. Cutters can be used to create hearts and stars, circles and triangles, numbers and flowers. Add the shapes immediately to the cake or leave to dry and prop up at angles on a dot of piped icing for an extra dimension.

Using plunger cutters offers a fail-safe way of stamping out tiny shapes, as the plunger gently pushes the icing shape out of the cutter easily every time.

Metal piping tubes can be used in a variety of ways to cut out shapes. The tips of large cream plain piping tubes, either 8 mm (⅜ inch), 5 mm (¼ inch) or 1 cm (½ inch), can be used to cut out small rounds as well as larger rounds using the upturned ends. Small piping tubes can be used to cut out tiny rounds, again using the upturned end.

To create crescent moon shapes, cut out rounds with biscuit cutters or piping tubes, then use the same cutter or tube to cut partially into each round to cut a crescent shape.

Shapes do not need to be solid. Try cutting a smaller shape from a larger one to make heart, star or circle frames, then leave empty or fill with a second coloured shape.

HOW TO MAKE A PIPING BAG

1 Cut a 25 cm (10 inch) square of greaseproof paper and fold in half to make a large triangle. Fold the triangle in half through the folded edge and pinch the second folded edge to mark the central fold.

2 Open out again. Holding the centre of the long folded edge towards you, curl the left-hand point of the triangle over to meet the centre pinch mark, forming a cone.

3 Next, bring the right-hand point over and around the cone so that the 3 points meet.

4 Lastly, fold the top points down several times to prevent the paper cone from unravelling.

TO USE THE BAG

Half-fill the bag with icing, fold the top edge down to enclose the icing, then snip off the tip. Make only a tiny snip, then squeeze out a little icing. Enlarge the hole with scissors if the piping needs to be larger. If using a metal piping tube, snip off the tip and drop the tube into the bag, enlarging the hole if needed so that it fits snugly with half the tube showing, then half-fill the bag with icing. For larger piping tubes, use a reusable fabric or plastic bag with a ready-cut tip.

MAKING FLOWERS

Specialist cake-icing shops sell a great range of fancy-shaped cutters, but you can easily be swept away with the choice. Try to go for shapes that you will use more than once, such as a set of different-sized flower plunger cutters or daisy cutters, rather than a single complicated orchid or rose.

To give added shape to flowers, press the flower out of the plunger cutter on to a piece of foam – a new foam washing-up sponge is ideal. This will curl the edges of the petals. Alternatively, curl the flowers on pieces of crumpled nonstick baking paper set in a bun tray. Once the flowers have been shaped, transfer them to a baking sheet lined with nonstick baking paper to harden.

If, when cutting flowers, the icing sticks to the cutter, then dip the cutter into a little icing sugar between use.

MAKING CHOCOLATE CURLS

These always look effective and are very simple to make, especially if the chocolate is at room temperature.

1 Turn a bar of chocolate over so that the smooth underside is uppermost. Position on the edge of a work surface.

2 Using a swivel-bladed vegetable peeler, pare away thin shavings of chocolate from the bar. If the curls are very small, warm the chocolate in a microwave oven for 10–15 seconds on High (if 650 watt) or Medium (if 700 watt) and try again.

3 For smaller, finer curls, grate the chocolate on to a plate instead using a medium or small grater setting.

WRAPPING CAKES WITH CHOCOLATE

This eye-catching but easy decoration is made by spreading melted chocolate on to a strip of nonstick baking paper that is a little taller than the side of your cake and long enough to wrap right around the outside of the cake. The secret is to melt the chocolate gently so that it stays glossy.

1 Bring a saucepan of water to the boil then set a large heatproof bowl over it so that it will heat up but not touch the water. Break the chocolate into the bowl, then remove the pan from the heat and leave for 5 minutes until the chocolate has melted.

2 Stir, then spread the chocolate over the strip of paper right up to one long edge and then make a wavy, jagged or swirly edge a little way down from the opposite long edge.

3 Press the chocolate on to the side of the cake so that the paper is on the outside, the soft chocolate is pressed against the cake and the decorative edge is uppermost.

4 Chill until set, then peel away the paper. Decorate the side of the cake with ribbon, if liked.

USING SWEETS AND CHOCOLATES

Adding brightly coloured sweets or chocolates to cakes creates maximum impact for minimum effort. These items can easily be used to give the effect of eyeballs (see page 36), spots (see page 90), jewels (see page 50), spider legs (see page 132), whiskers (see page 62) or simple lines of colour (see page 80).

USING CANDLES

For very young children, it just wouldn't be a birthday cake without a candle to mark each year of their age. Look out for pastel- or primary-coloured ones, dotty or glittery ones, shaped, wiggly or wand-like ones, numerical candles, those that spell 'happy birthday' or even those that will not blow out! Add candles to candleholders to catch the melting wax or make your own with tiny balls or shapes of ready-to-roll icing.

Tiny tots

Cheeky pirate

serves 10
decoration time 1 hour

double quantity Butter Icing (see page 21)

pink paste food colouring

Large round Quick-mix Sandwich Cake (see page 14)

23 cm (9 inch) thin round cake board or plate

250 g (8 oz) red ready-to-roll icing

sifted icing sugar, for dusting

75 g (3 oz) white ready-to-roll icing

1 round blue liquorice sweet

50 g (2 oz) royal blue ready-to-roll icing

25 g (1 oz) black ready-to-roll icing

1 gold foil-covered coin

Tip

The bandanna colours can be varied according to the colours of icing that you happen to have. For example, use a combination of blue, green and white, or green, yellow and brown.

1 Colour the butter icing pale pink with the colouring, then use some of the icing to sandwich the cakes together. Put on to the cake board or plate. Reserve 2 teaspoons of the butter icing and spread the remainder over the top and side of the cake, smoothing with a small palette knife.

2 Knead the red icing on a surface lightly dusted with icing sugar until slightly softened. Roll out until a little larger than half the cake top. Cut a straight edge with a knife. Drape the icing over the cake so that the cut edge covers one-third of the cake top in a diagonal line, draping downwards on the right-hand side of the cake to the cake board, and add a few pleats to resemble a bandanna. Trim off the excess.

3 Re-knead and roll out the trimmings. Cut out a mouth shape and 2 very thin strips for the ends of the mouth and press in place on the cake.

4 Knead and roll out the white icing. Cut out small rounds using the upturned end of a piping tube and press these at intervals on to the bandanna, sticking them in place with a little water. Roll a small white icing ball, then flatten, shape into an oval eye and press on to the pirate's face. Add the blue sweet for the eyeball and stick in place with a tiny dot of the reserved butter icing. Colour the remaining white icing pale pink with the colouring and shape into an ear. Press on to the side of the cake.

5 Knead and roll out the blue icing. Cut out more spots for the bandanna. Knead and roll out the black icing. Cut out a semicircle for an eyepatch. Shape the remaining black icing into a thin rope and press above the eyepatch, across the face and over the ear. Add a gold coin earring and stick in place with a dot of butter icing.

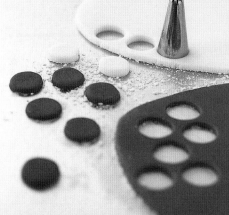

King of the road

serves 20
decoration time 45 minutes

1 Trim the top of the cake level, if needed. Cut the cake horizontally in half, then sandwich back together with most of the butter icing. Put on to the cake board or plate. Spread the top and side very thinly with the remaining butter icing.

2 Cut off 200 g (7 oz) of the white icing, wrap and reserve. Knead the remaining icing, roll out and use to cover the top and sides of the cake and the cake board. Smooth with the fingertips, trim off the excess and wrap the trimmings.

3 Colour the 200 g (7 oz) reserved white icing pale grey with a little of the black colouring. Shape three-quarters of the grey into a long rope 46 cm (18 inches) long, then flatten it into a strip 3.5 cm (1½ inches) wide with a rolling pin. Straighten one long edge, then cut the opposite edge into a wavy line. Position around the lower side of the cake, wavy edge uppermost, sticking it in place with a little water, if necessary. Trim off the excess. Knead and roll out the reserved grey icing and cut out a winding road and stick on to the cake top with a little water. Colour the trimmings black, wrap and reserve.

4 Knead and roll out the red icing and cut out 2 cars 7 cm (3 inches) long. Knead and roll out the blue icing and cut out 2 lorries of similar size. Press on to the cake, leaving space for the yellow cars. Knead and roll out a little yellow icing, cut out 2 cars and press into the spaces. Roll small black balls then flatten for wheels. Press on to the cars, sticking in place with water.

5 Shape a larger 3-D car from the remaining yellow icing and position on the road, standing on pieces of icing trimmings, then cover these with black wheels. Roll out the white icing trimmings, cut out small shapes for car windows and add. Roll small balls and press on for headlights. Add tiny white strips for road markings. Cut very thin strips from any remaining red and black icing, trim and press on to the large yellow car bonnet and boot. Add lollipop road signs.

23 cm (9 inch) deep round Large Madeira Cake (see page 13)

one-and-a-half quantity Butter Icing (see page 21)

28 cm (11 inch) thin round cake board or plate

700 g (1 lb 7 oz) white ready-to-roll icing

sifted icing sugar, for dusting

black paste food colouring

75 g (3 oz) red ready-to-roll icing

75 g (3 oz) blue ready-to-roll icing

175 g (6 oz) yellow ready-to-roll icing

2 red lollipops, unwrapped

Tips

- For a child who may be getting a toy race track for a birthday present, use a little more grey icing and make it into a circular roadway on top of the cake.
- Use any remaining icing trimmings to make additional road signs by covering cocktail sticks with ropes of icing then adding flattened balls of coloured icing. Leave to dry flat on nonstick baking paper, then pipe on details – perhaps the child's age or name – with tubes of writing icing.

Magic numbers

serves 8
decoration time 45 minutes

8 cm (7 inch) deep round Small Madeira Cake
(see page 12)

single quantity Butter Icing (see page 21)

20 cm (8 inch) thin round cake board or plate

400 g (13 oz) white ready-to-roll icing

sifted icing sugar, for dusting

blue paste food colouring

125 g (4 oz) yellow ready-to-roll icing

125 g (4 oz) red ready-to-roll icing

125 g (4 oz) orange ready-to-roll icing

Tips

- Adjust the sum to relate to the age of the particular individual – this is a great cake for all ages, including bigger birthdays such as 18, 40 or even 80!
- Boxed sets of small number cutters can be bought from good cookware shops, cookware departments in large department stores or specialist cake-icing shops.

1 Cut the cake horizontally in half, then sandwich back together with most of the butter icing. Put on to the cake board or plate. Spread the top and side very thinly with the remaining butter icing.

2 Knead the white icing on a surface lightly dusted with icing sugar until slightly softened. Roll out and use to cover the cake. Smooth in place with your fingertips dusted with icing sugar, then trim off the excess.

3 Colour the trimmings bright blue with the food colouring and knead until an even colour. Wrap and reserve.

4 Knead and roll out a little of the yellow icing and cut out a number 2 and different-sized stars with small cutters. Knead and roll out some red icing and cut out a number 3 and some stars. Knead and roll out some of the orange icing and cut out some number 5s and some stars.

5 Arrange the yellow 2, the red 3 and one orange 5 on top of the cake, leaving spaces in between. Stick coloured stars randomly over the cake top with a little water.

6 Roll out the reserved blue icing, cut some small narrow strips and press on to the cake top between the numbers for plus and equals signs. Stamp out a few tiny stars and press on to the cake top, then cut out large stars from the remaining blue.

7 Stick the large blue stars around the side of the cake, leaving spaces in between for numbers. Add alternate-coloured 5s to the spaces, using the orange 5s you cut out earlier and re-kneading and rolling out the rest of the icing trimmings to cut 5s from other colours, as necessary.

Alien invasion

serves 6
decoration time 45 minutes

6 Muffins (see page 17) or bought large
   muffins, paper cases removed

single quantity vanilla-flavoured Butter Icing
   (see page 21)

selection of liquorice or fruit sweets

150 g (5 oz) bright pink ready-to-roll icing

sifted icing sugar, for dusting

large round plate

150 g (5 oz) blue ready-to-roll icing

150 g (5 oz) green ready-to-roll icing

2 black liquorice Catherine wheels

1   Stand the muffins on a chopping board and spread the butter icing over the tops and sides to cover. Press on the liquorice or fruit sweets for eyes and noses.

2   Knead the pink icing on a surface lightly dusted with icing sugar until slightly softened. Roll out thinly and cut narrow strips. Drape the strips randomly over the tops of 2 muffins so that they cover the butter icing and extend down and over the work surface. Carefully transfer to a large round plate.

3   Repeat with each of the remaining pieces of different-coloured icing until each of the 6 muffins has been covered with the different-coloured strips.

4   To complete, press pieces of unwound Catherine wheel into the top of the muffins for antennae.

Tip

Let your imagination run riot and add whacky coloured feet, mouths or ears made out of icing or sweets.

High flyer

serves 12
decoration time 1 hour

30 x 23 x 5 cm (12 x 9 x 2 inch) roasting tin
    Medium Madeira Cake (see page 13)

one-and-a-half quantity Butter Icing
    (see page 21)

25 x 35 cm (10 x 14 inch) rectangular cake
    board, covered with 500 g (1 lb) pale blue
    ready-to-roll icing, or similar-sized glass
    chopping board

500 g (1 lb) white ready-to-roll icing

sifted icing sugar, for dusting

375 g (12 oz) red ready-to-roll icing

75 g (3 oz) grey ready-to-roll icing

2 black and white liquorice sweets, 1 halved,
    1 quartered

Tips

- Although this design is for a young
  child, the colours could be changed
  and easily adapted to make a Spitfire,
  Mosquito or other plane for a model-
  making enthusiast. Borrow the kit box
  for reference for the correct colours
  and markings.
- If the liquorice sweets are too heavy to
  stick, use the remaining butter icing from
  the edge of the bowl as glue.

1 Put the cake top downwards on a chopping board with
a narrow edge nearest you. Cut a 12.5 cm (5 inch) strip
the length of the longest side for the plane body. Cut the
remaining piece in half through the longest edge. Reserve
one piece for wings. Cut a 2 cm (¾ inch) strip off the side of
the remaining piece. Reserve for the top tail fin. Put the last
piece on to the plane body and shape into the cockpit,
rounding off the front, tapering the back and sides and
sloping the roof. Curve the edges of the plane.

2 Cut the reserved wing cake horizontally in half to form
2 thinner wings. Shape the tips and cut a slim diagonal slice
off the other side to butt against the body of the plane.

3 Stick all the plane body parts together with butter icing,
keeping the wings and tail fin separate. Spread the outside
thinly with butter icing, then the wings and tail fin. Lift the
body on to the cake or chopping board to sit diagonally.

4 Knead and roll out the white icing to 33 x 23 cm (13 x 9
inches), drape over the cake and smooth in place. Trim off the
excess. Re-knead, roll out and cover the top tail fin. Cut the side
tail detail from the icing trimmings and stick in place with water.

5 Knead and roll out one-third of the red icing and cut 2 strips
30 x 2.5 cm (12 x 1 inch) then press around the base of the
plane, butting up to the side tail detail and front nose cone.
Cut a curved strip for the nose cone and stick in place. Use
the remaining red icing to cover the wings. Butt them against
the plane body. Cut the top tail fin details from the trimmings.

6 Knead and roll out the grey icing and cut a semicircle for the
front window and round side windows and stick in place. Cut
strips for the wing and fin details. Stick 2 sweet quarters in
front of each wing and a halved sweet to each side of the tail.

space ship

serves 10
decoration time 1 hour

1 Cut the sandwich cake horizontally in half. Level the basin cake top, if necessary, then cut horizontally in half. Sandwich both cakes back together with some of the butter icing. Spread the top of the sandwich cake with some of the butter icing and put the basin cake, trimmed top downwards, on top.

2 Transfer the cake stack to the smaller cake board and spread the remaining butter icing thinly all over the top and sides.

3 Knead the white icing on a surface lightly dusted with icing sugar until slightly softened. Roll out to a 30 cm (12 inch) round. Lift over the cake with a rolling pin, smooth in place and trim off the excess. Stand the cake stack on a saucer or lid on the icing-covered larger cake board or plate so that it is raised slightly above it.

4 Reknead and roll out the icing trimmings. Cut out tiny stars with a mini cutter. Cut out rounds in 2 sizes using the upturned end of a small- and medium-sized piping tube, then cut part way through the larger rounds to create crescent moon shapes. Add the flying saucer sweets to the board or plate, reserving one.

5 Stick the round blue liquorice sweets and white chocolate buttons alternately around the side of the bottom cake with piped dots of royal or writing icing.

6 Stick the green twisted bootlaces around the base of the top cake with piped dots of icing. Stick candy-covered chocolate drops above, adding 2 blue, then a green. Stick jelly sweets in a line above, adding 2 orange, then a green.

7 Decorate the top of the space ship with lollipops. Add the reserved flying saucer, with the square liquorice sweet and an offcut of bootlace, cut side uppermost, on top, securing with piped dots of royal or writing icing.

Large single Quick-mix sandwich cake (see page 14) and 900 ml (1½ pint) pudding basin Medium Madeira Cake (see page 13)

one-and-a-half-quantity Butter Icing (see page 21)

20 cm (8 inch) thin round cake board

500 g (1 lb) white ready-to-roll icing

sifted icing sugar, for dusting

saucer or jam jar lid

30 cm (12 inch) thin round cake board, covered with 375 g (12 oz) deep blue ready-to-roll icing, or a large blue plate

flying saucer sherbet sweets

14 round blue and 1 square orange liquorice sweets

14 white chocolate rainbow buttons

2 tablespoons Royal Icing (see page 25) or 1 tube white writing icing

4 green apple-flavoured twisted bootlaces, cut to short lengths

20 blue and 11 green candy-covered chocolate drops

7 mixed lime green, yellow and orange lollipops

18 orange and 10 green jelly sweets

Tip

Vary the sweets according to your child's particular preferences. Look out for fruity versions of liquorice sweets too.

Knight's castle

serves 24
decoration time 1 hour

20 cm (8 inch) deep square chocolate-flavoured
   Large Madeira Cake (see page 13)

one-and-a-half quantity chocolate-flavoured
   Butter Icing (see page 21)

25 cm (10 inch) thin square cake board, covered
   with 200 g (7 oz) black ready-to-roll icing, or
   plate

1 kg (2 lb) white ready-to-roll icing

sifted icing sugar, for dusting

black paste food colouring

28 cm (11 inch) chocolate-flavoured Swiss Roll
   (see page 18) or 23 cm (9 inch) bought
   chocolate Swiss roll

400 g (13 oz) deep blue ready-to-roll icing

little Royal Icing (see page 25), coloured grey

little Royal Icing (see page 25), coloured black or
   tube black writing icing

4 chocolate sticks

25 g (1 oz) yellow ready-to-roll icing

25 g (1 oz) green ready-to-roll icing

Tips

• If you are short of time, then use bought
  cocktail stick flags for the pennants on
  the turret tops.
• If you choose to bake your own Swiss roll
  for this cake from the recipe on page 18
  you will find you have quite a bit to spare
  after making the turrets and gate tower.
  This can be eaten as a cook's perk!

1 Trim the top of the cake level, if needed. Cut the cake horizontally in half and sandwich back together with some of the butter icing. Reserve 4 tablespoons of the butter icing and spread the remainder thinly over the top and sides. Place on the cake board or plate.

2 Knead the white icing, then colour grey with the black colouring until partially mixed and mottled.

3 Wrap and reserve 150 g (5 oz) of the grey icing. Use the remainder to cover the cake. Trim off the excess and reserve.

4 Cut the Swiss roll into four 5 cm (2 inch) thick slices for turrets and one 2.5 cm (1 inch) thick slice. Cut the latter in half and use one half for the gate tower. Spread the top and sides of the Swiss roll pieces with most of the remaining butter icing.

5 Roll out the remaining grey icing in batches. Cut four 6 cm (2½ inch) plain rounds with a biscuit cutter and press on to the turret tops. Cut four 5 x 23 cm (2 x 9 inch) pieces and cover the turret sides. Cover the gate tower with a smaller piece. Reserve any trimmings. Stick the Swiss roll pieces in place with the last of the butter icing.

6 Knead and shape half the blue icing into a rope 1.5 cm (¾ inch) thick. Cut into 1.5 cm (¾ inch) wide slices and cut every other one in half. Stick these alternate-sized 'bricks' around the fort top and the turret tops with a little piped grey royal icing. Repeat until all the top edges are covered. Cut a blue door from the trimmings. Stick on to the fort front.

7 Colour the remaining grey ready-to-roll icing black. Roll out, cut large and smaller squares. Stick around the door and corners of the castle with grey piped icing. Pipe on a black portcullis. Press chocolate sticks into the turrets. Roll out the yellow and green ready-to-roll icing, cut flags and attach.

Fairy princess crowns

serves 12
decoration time 45 minutes, plus drying

single quantity Butter Icing (see page 21)

pink paste food colouring

12 Fairy Cakes (see page 16) or bought fairy
   cakes, paper cases removed

500 g (1 lb) pale pink ready-to-roll icing

sifted icing sugar, for dusting

mauve sugar sprinkles

blue and pink icing shapes

red jelly diamonds

1 tube fine white or pink writing icing or little
   Royal Icing (see page 25)

large round or square plate

1 Colour the butter icing pale pink with the food colouring.
Trim the tops of cakes level, if needed, then turn each cake
top downwards and spread the butter icing over the new
tops and sides.

2 Knead the pink ready-to-roll icing on a surface lightly
dusted with icing sugar until slightly softened. Roll out one-
third and cut 3 strips 20 x 5 cm (8 x 2 inches) long. Using
the upturned end of a large cream plain piping tube, cut a
scalloped edge along one of the long edges. Repeat on
the other 2 icing strips.

3 Press an icing strip, scalloped edge uppermost, around one
cake to form a crown, trimming off the excess and reserving.
Press the tips of the crown upright – if they are very floppy,
trim a little off the tips. Use the trimmings to make a fourth
crown then continue with the remaining icing. Repeat until all
12 crowns have been made.

4 Spoon the mauve sprinkles inside each crown, then decorate
the sides with icing shapes and jelly diamonds, sticking them
in place with dots of piped writing or royal icing. Transfer the
crowns to a plate. Leave for 30 minutes in a cool place for
the icing to harden.

Tip
Look out for tubs of different-coloured
sprinkles and tiny sugar decorations.
Each tub is divided into five or six sections,
each containing a toning sprinkle or icing
sugar decoration.

Daisy chain

serves 10
decoration time 1 hour, plus drying

Large round Quick-mix Sandwich Cake (see
   page 14)

single quantity Butter Icing (see page 21)

25 cm (10 inch) thin round cake board,
   covered with 375 g (12 oz) white ready-to-
   roll icing, or plate

500 g (1 lb) pale yellow ready-to-roll icing

sifted icing sugar, for dusting

white vegetable fat, for greasing

50 g (2 oz) white flower paste (see tip, below)

3 tablespoons Royal Icing (see page 25),
   coloured pale green

1 tablespoon Royal Icing (see page 25),
   coloured yellow, or 1 tube yellow writing
   icing

1 metre (39 inches) x 2 cm (¾ inch) wide pale
   green chiffon ribbon

Tips

• Make sure that you bake the cakes in
  straight-sided rather than sloping tins for
  a smooth-sided finish.
• Flower paste can be bought from
  specialist cake-icing shops and can be
  rolled very much more thinly than
  ordinary ready-to-roll icing.

1 Sandwich the cakes together with some of the butter icing.
Transfer to the cake board or plate. Reserve 1 teaspoon of
the butter icing and spread the remainder thinly over the top
and side of the cake.

2 Knead the yellow ready-to-roll icing on a surface lightly
dusted with icing sugar until slightly softened. Roll out and use
to cover the cake. Smooth the top and side with your fingers
dusted with icing sugar. Trim off the excess.

3 To make the flowers, rub a little vegetable fat over a
chopping board, rolling pin and base of a 2.5 cm (1 inch)
and 2 cm (¾ inch) plastic daisy cutter. Cut off half the flower
paste, wrap and reserve. Roll out the remaining flower paste
thinly. Stamp out a few flower shapes at a time and lift off
the board with a small knife on to pieces of crumpled
nonstick baking paper to shape. Leave to dry for 30
minutes. Continue stamping, re-kneading and rolling out
the trimmings, and using the reserved flower paste, until it
has all been used up.

4 Spoon the pale green royal icing into a greaseproof paper
piping bag (see page 31), snip off the tip and pipe a swirly
line over the top and slightly over the side of the cake for a
daisy stem. Stick the flowers at intervals over the piped stem,
adding some to the base of the cake board with dots of
green piped icing.

5 Pipe dots of yellow icing in the centres of the flowers. Tie the
ribbon in a bow around the side of the cake and trim off the
excess ribbon.

Sunflower cup cakes

serves 12
decoration time 30 minutes

1 Trim the tops of the fairy cakes level, if needed. Divide the butter icing between the tops of the cakes then spread into an even layer.

2 Knead the yellow icing on a surface lightly dusted with icing sugar until slightly softened. Roll out and cut into 2.5 cm (1 inch) wide strips. Cut each strip into triangular-shaped petals and stick around the edge of each cake.

3 Add a second row of icing petals, a little in from the first, re-rolling the trimmings as needed. Knead and roll out the brown icing and cut out 2.5 cm (1 inch) circles with a fluted cutter. Press into the centre of each flower.

4 Pipe on red mouths and black eyes with writing icing. Arrange the cakes on the plate.

single quantity Butter Icing (see page 21)

12 Fairy Cakes (see page 16), with green foil paper cases

250 g (8 oz) yellow ready-to-roll icing

sifted icing sugar, for dusting

125 g (4 oz) brown ready-to-roll icing

1 tube red writing icing

1 tube black writing icing

large green plate

Tip
Chocolate sweets or jumbo chocolate buttons could be used for the flower faces, if preferred.

Mini birthday cakes

serves 12
decoration time 20 minutes, plus drying

single quantity Glacé Icing (see page 24)

mauve paste food colouring

pink or red paste food colouring

yellow paste food colouring

12 Fairy Cakes (see page 16), with white paper cases, or bought fairy cakes

4 each of yellow and white, pink, mauve and white candles

75 g (3 oz) dolly mixture sweets

75 g (3 oz) candy-covered chocolate drops

large round or square plate

1 Put one-third of the glacé icing into a separate bowl and colour lilac with a little mauve colouring. Spoon half the remaining icing into another bowl and colour pale pink with the pink colouring or with a little of the red colouring. Colour the remaining icing pale yellow.

2 Spoon the yellow icing over 4 of the fairy cakes, the lilac icing over another 4 and the pink icing over the remaining cakes, smoothing in place with the back of the spoon.

3 Add a yellow and white candle to the centre of each yellow iced cake, then press co-ordinating-coloured sweets around the base of each candle. Repeat with the correspondingly coloured candles and sweets for the remaining cakes. Transfer the cakes to a plate. Leave in a cool place for the icing to set for 30 minutes before serving.

Tip

For chocolate fans, cover chocolate-flavoured fairy cakes with Chocolate Fudge Icing (see page 22), brightly-coloured sweets and candy-covered chocolate drops.

Noughts and crosses

serves 9
decoration time 20 minutes, plus drying

150 g (5 oz) red ready-to-roll icing

sifted icing sugar, for dusting

150 g (5 oz) yellow ready-to-roll icing

9 Fairy Cakes (see page 16) or bought fairy cakes

single quantity Butter Icing (see page 21)

20 cm (12 inch) square plate or thin cake board

7 wide strawberry-flavoured jelly strips

1 Make a cross template by cutting a rectangle 6 x 5 cm (2½ x 2 inches) from paper or cardboard, then cut out a small triangle from the centre of each long side and a larger triangle from each of the short sides.

2 Knead the red icing on a surface lightly dusted with icing sugar until slightly softened. Roll out and cut around the template to make 5 crosses. Put on to a baking sheet lined with nonstick baking paper lightly dusted with icing sugar.

3 Knead and roll out the yellow icing and cut out 4 rounds with a 5 cm (2 inch) plain biscuit cutter. Stamp out a small circle from the centre of each round using the tip of a large cream piping tube or an upturned icing piping tube. Add to the baking sheet and leave to dry for at least 1 hour.

4 Spread the butter icing over the centre of the fairy cakes and top with the dried icing shapes. Arrange on the plate or cake board with a grid made from the jelly strips, cut into appropriate lengths and overlapped as shown.

Tip

This idea could easily be adapted to make a crossword with stamped-out letters on a larger jelly-strip grid.

Magician's hat

serves 16
decoration time 1 hour

1 Trim the tops of the chocolate cakes level, if needed, then sandwich them together with some of the butter icing. Spread a little of the remaining butter icing over the side, filling in any gaps where the cakes join. Put on to the icing-covered cake board or plate.

2 Knead the black icing on a surface lightly dusted with icing sugar until slightly softened. Roll out and cut a strip 55 x 15 cm (22 x 6 inches) or long and tall enough to go around the side of the cake stack. Carefully lift the icing and press on to the cake stack side. Trim off the excess, wrap and reserve.

3 Spread the uncovered cake board with a little butter icing. Knead and roll out the grey icing and use to cover the top of the board. Roll out the reserved black icing into a strip 73 x 3.5 cm (29 x 1½ inches) and press on to the edge of the board for the hat rim, trimming off the excess. Stick the cake board on to the cake stack top with some butter icing.

4 For the rabbit, cover the muffin with butter icing and stick in place on the cake top with butter icing. Cut a thin diagonal slice off each sponge roll and position on the cake for ears and paws, securing the ears with cocktail sticks for extra support, if necessary. Spread these with butter icing.

5 Knead and roll out the pink icing, cut out ear and paw pads and press in place. Form a U-shaped mouth and press in place.

6 Add dolly mixture eyes and nose, pressing liquorice bootlace whiskers under the nose. Stick rainbow pearl eyeballs to the eyes with a little butter icing. Knead and roll out the white icing, cut out large and small stars and stick to the hat with the remaining butter icing. Leave the icing to harden for a few hours before serving.

2 x 18 cm (7 inch) deep round chocolate-flavoured Small Madeira Cakes (see page 12)

double quantity Butter Icing (see page 21)

23 cm (9 inch) thin round cake board, covered with 375 g (12 oz) mauve ready-to-roll icing, or coloured plate

625 g (1¼ lb) black ready-to-roll icing

sifted icing sugar, for dusting

125 g (4 oz) grey ready-to-roll icing

23 cm (9 inch) thin round cake board

1 muffin (see page 17) or bought muffin, paper case removed

4 bought mini chocolate, jam or vanilla sponge rolls

50 g (2 oz) pink ready-to-roll icing

1 round dolly mixture sweet, halved

1 pink square dolly mixture sweet

small piece black liquorice bootlace, snipped into short lengths

2 pink rainbow pearls

75 g (3 oz) white ready-to-roll icing

Tip

Short of time? Then use three 30 cm (6 inch) shop-bought chocolate sandwich cakes and a bought muffin and roll out black icing to fit the height and circumference of the cake stack.

Bunch of balloons

serves 8
decoration time 45 minutes

18 cm (7 inch) deep round Small Madeira
    Cake (see page 12)

single quantity Butter Icing (see page 21)

20 cm (8 inch) thin round cake board or plate

400 g (13 oz) orange ready-to-roll icing

sifted icing sugar, for dusting

25 g (1 oz) red ready-to-roll icing

25 g (1 oz) deep blue ready-to-roll icing

25 g (1 oz) yellow ready-to-roll icing

75 g (3 oz) white ready-to-roll icing

selection of different-coloured narrow ribbons

1 Trim the top of the cake, if needed, then cut the cake horizontally in half and sandwich back together with some of the butter icing. Put on to the cake board or plate. Reserve 2 teaspoons of the butter icing and spread the remainder thinly over the top and side.

2 Knead the orange icing on a surface lightly dusted with icing sugar until slightly softened. Roll out and use to cover the cake, smoothing in place with your fingertips dusted with icing sugar. Trim off the excess, wrap and reserve.

3 Knead and roll out the red icing, cut out 2 balloon shapes and arrange on the cake top, with a piece of ribbon, about 15 cm (6 inches) long, tucked under each balloon. Repeat with the blue and yellow, then make one balloon with the white icing. Tie the balloon ribbons together with another ribbon, then trim the ends diagonally with scissors.

4 Shape the remaining white icing into a rope about 58 cm (23 inches) long. Repeat with the reserved orange icing, then twist the ropes together and press on to the base of the cake board, sticking in place with the reserved butter icing.

Tip

Vary the colours of the balloons and cake to suit your child's favourite colours. You might also like to pipe on your child's name, piping a letter on to each balloon.

Sweet-guzzling monster

serves 20
decoration time 50 minutes, plus drying

1.5 litre (2½ pint) pudding basin Medium
   Madeira Cake (see page 13)

18 cm (7 inch) deep round Small Madeira
   Cake (see page 12)

one-and-a-half quantity Butter Icing
   (see page 21)

25 cm (10 inch) thick round silver cake board
   or plate

750 g (1½ lb) white ready-to-roll icing

sifted icing sugar, for dusting

green paste food colouring

100 g (3½ oz) pale pink ready-to-roll icing

125 g (4 oz) purple ready-to-roll icing

15 g (½ oz) white ready-to-roll icing

selection of sweets and lollipops

1 Level the basin cake top, if needed. Cut each cake horizontally in half and sandwich back together with butter icing. Spread the top of the round cake with butter icing, then transfer to the cake board or plate, positioning the cake slightly off-centre close to the side of the cake board. Press the basin cake, trimmed top downwards, on top.

2 Reserve 2 teaspoons of the butter icing and spread the rest over the cake top and sides.

3 Knead the white icing on a surface lightly dusted with icing sugar until slightly softened. Knead in a little green colouring until partially mixed and faintly marbled. Roll out into a 35 cm (14 inch) round. Lift on the rolling pin and drape over the cake so that it falls in folds, easing it down to the board with your fingertips, if necessary. Leave space between the front folds for the mouth.

4 Knead and roll out the pink icing thickly. Cut out 2 feet and tuck under the front of the green icing. Roll out the icing a little thinner and cut out an oval-shaped mouth 10 x 7 cm (4 x 3 inches). Stick in place with a little water. Reserve trimmings for hands.

5 Knead and roll out one-third of the purple icing into a rope 12 cm (5 inches) long for the top lip, pinch together in 2 places, then stick on to the mouth with a little of the reserved butter icing. Cut out an oval 12 x 7 cm (5 x 3 inches) from the remaining purple icing, dot the lower underside edges with butter icing and stick on to the mouth to create a pouch.

6 Shape the purple icing trimmings into 2 arched eyebrows and 2 eyeballs. Shape the white icing into 2 eyes. Stick the features in place with water or butter icing. Cut out hands from the reserved pink icing and stick to the front of the cake. Leave to dry for at least 30 minutes, then add sweets to the mouth.

Tip

To make a spooky Halloween version, cover the cake in white icing and add ghoulish black lips, eyeballs and eyebrows.

Older kids

Grand master

serves 20
decoration time 1 hour

20 cm (8 inch) deep square Large Madeira
    Cake (see page 13)

one-and-a-half quantity Butter Icing
    (see page 21)

23 cm (9 inch) thin square cake board or plate

1 kg (2 lb) white ready-to-roll icing

sifted icing sugar, for dusting

125 g (4 oz) dark blue ready-to-roll icing

125 g (4 oz) black ready-to-roll icing

1.25 metres (49 inches) x 2.5 cm (1 inch) wide
    blue and white checked ribbon

Tip

As the chess pieces are relatively time-
consuming to make, don't attempt to make
a full set, but give the impression that a
game is halfway through, with some of the
pieces already taken.

1 Level the top of the cake, if needed. Cut the cake horizontally
in half and sandwich back together with some of the butter
icing. Put on to the cake board or plate and spread the
remaining butter icing thinly over the top and sides.

2 Cut off 125 g (4 oz) of the white icing, wrap and reserve.
Knead the remainder on a surface lightly dusted with icing
sugar until slightly softened. Roll out and use to cover the
top and sides of the cake, smoothing in place with your
fingertips dusted with icing sugar. Trim off the excess and
add to the reserved white icing.

3 Knead and roll out the blue icing thinly to 10 x 20 cm
(4 x 8 inches). Cut vertically into eight 2.5 cm (1 inch) wide
strips, then cut horizontally into 4 equal-sized strips to make
32 squares. Arrange these on top of the cake in a
chequerboard pattern with 4 in each row.

4 Make stylized chess pieces from the reserved white icing
and the black icing based on different-sized triangles of
icing, adding tiny flattened balls of icing and rounded balls
of different sizes for the pawns, bishop, king and queen.
Make a diagonal cut in the top of the bishop. Add different-
shaped crowns to the king and queen and tiny castellated
strips to the rook or castle. For the knight, add an oval head
and cut a small strip with one side cut into a thin fringe for
the mane. Add ears and stand on a small plinth.

5 Arrange the chess pieces on the cake to look as if a game is
in progress, with a few pieces beside the cake board. Tie
the ribbon around the side of the cake.

Rock fan

serves 12
decoration time 1 hour

1 Put the roasting tin cake, base uppermost, on to a large chopping board with the Swiss roll butted up against one of the short edges. Trim the large cake to resemble a guitar body (see picture opposite). Cut a guitar head from the cake trimmings.

2 Cut the guitar shape horizontally in half and sandwich back together with some of the butter icing. Transfer to the cake board or tray, leaving space for the guitar 'neck'. Spread the top and sides thinly with more butter icing and spread the rest over the head.

3 Knead the coffee-coloured icing, roll out and use to cover the top of the guitar. Trim off the excess. Knead and roll out three-quarters of the dark brown icing and cut two strips each 23 x 5 cm (9 x 2 inches). Press around the sides of the guitar, butting the edges together at the top and bottom. Roll out and cover the head with the remainder. Add the Swiss roll neck and the shaped head to the cake board or tray.

4 Knead and roll out the white icing. Cut out a rectangle 18 x 12 cm (7 x 5 inches), then shape as in the picture. Press on to the guitar body. Cut 3 small string rests and 3 volume control knobs from the trimmings and press on. Cut a piece for the top of the head. Shape small balls of icing for string tighteners. Stick in place.

5 Roll out thin ropes of white icing and stick on to the Swiss roll at intervals, adding flattened balls of icing in between with piped white icing. Pipe dots of icing over the string rests and add 6 silver balls to each.

6 Tie lengths of silver cord around the string tighteners and secure on the guitar with balls of icing. Snip off the excess and cover with a thick rectangular strip of white icing. Knead, roll out and cut black musical icing notes to decorate the board or tray.

30 x 23 x 5 cm (12 x 9 x 2 inch) roasting tin chocolate-flavoured Medium Madeira Cake (see page 13)

28 cm (11 inch) chocolate-flavoured Swiss Roll (see page 18) or 28 cm (11 inch) bought chocolate Swiss roll

single quantity chocolate-flavoured Butter Icing (see page 21)

62 x 25 cm (25 x 10 inch) thin silver cake board or larger coloured tray

375 g (12 oz) coffee-coloured ready-to-roll icing

sifted icing sugar, for dusting

375 g (12 oz) dark brown ready-to-roll icing

250 g (8 oz) white ready-to-roll icing

2 tablespoons Royal Icing (see page 25)

18 edible silver balls

4 metres (13 feet) fine silver cord

125 g (4 oz) black ready-to-roll icing

Tips

- The cake or chopping board required is such an unusual size that you may prefer to serve the cake on a large plastic tray instead and cover it with foil or coloured foil wrapping paper.
- If you find that the cord for the guitar strings keeps unravelling, secure it around a halved cocktail stick, then cover this with icing, but make sure to remove it before cutting the cake.

Soccer star

serves 10
decoration time 1 hour

2 x 900 ml (1½ pint) pudding basin Medium
  Madeira Cakes (see page 13)

single quantity Butter Icing (see page 21)

500 g (1 lb) white ready-to-roll icing

sifted icing sugar, for dusting

23 cm (9 inch) thin cake board or round plate

125 g (4 oz) black ready-to-roll icing

100 g (3½ oz) blue ready-to-roll icing (or
  colour of your child's favourite team)

1 tube coloured writing icing (optional)

Tips

- Roll out extra icing for the hexagons as
  necessary, keeping the remainder well
  wrapped to prevent it from drying out
  and making shaping difficult.
- The top of a spice jar makes an ideal
  circle template for the first stage of
  making the hexagon template.
- If using a cake board, you may like
  to cover it with green butter icing or
  green-coloured desiccated coconut to
  resemble grass.

1 Level the basin cake tops, if necessary, and sandwich
together with some of the butter icing to form a ball shape.
Reserve 1 tablespoon of the remaining butter icing and
spread the remainder thinly over the outside of the cake.

2 Knead and roll out two-thirds of the white icing thinly. Use to
cover the cake, smoothing with your fingertips dusted with
icing sugar. Trim off the excess, wrap and reserve. Transfer
the cake to the cake board or plate.

3 Create a hexagon template by cutting a 3.5 cm (1½ inch)
round from greaseproof paper. Fold the round in half, then
fold the half into 3. Cut a straight line between the ends of
the fold lines, then open out.

4 Knead and roll out a little of the black icing and cut out a
black hexagon. Press on to the cake top. Roll out a little of
the reserved white trimmings and cut out white hexagons,
arrange these around the black one and press or nudge the
shapes so that they fit exactly. Add a row of black hexagons,
then more white hexagons, sticking in place down the sides
of the ball with dots of the reserved butter icing. As you cover
more of the cake, you may need to trim down the hexagon
shapes slightly to fit. Reserve a little white icing.

5 Knead and roll out the blue icing and cut out 3 rounds of
decreasing size with fluted biscuit cutters, the largest 7 cm
(3 inches). Frill the edges by rolling a cocktail stick back and
forth over them. Press one on top of the other for the rosette.
Add a small round of the reserved white icing to the centre.
Cut strips of the blue icing for the rosette tails. Arrange the
rosette by the side of the football. Pipe your child's name or
age on to the centre of the rosette, if liked.

Speedy skater

serves 6
decoration time 45 minutes

4 chocolate-covered marshmallow teacakes

28 cm (11 inch) chocolate-flavoured Swiss Roll
(see page 18) or 28 cm (11 inch) bought
chocolate Swiss roll

25 cm (10 inch) thin square cake board,
covered with 250 g (8 oz) white or mauve
ready-to-roll icing, or mauve plate

2 tablespoons apricot jam

single quantity Chocolate Fudge Icing (see
page 22)

100 g (3½ oz) yellow ready-to-roll icing

sifted icing sugar, for dusting

75 g (3 oz) black ready-to-roll icing

250 g (8 oz) grey ready-to-roll icing

Tips

- If you are planning to give some skates
  as a birthday present, then adapt the
  colours on the cake to match them.
- If you are putting the cake on an icing-
  covered board, you may find it easier
  to spread the Swiss roll with fudge icing
  before you move it to the cake board.
- For a smooth finish to the chocolate
  fudge icing, use a small palette knife
  dipped into boiling water when
  smoothing it.

1 Put the teacakes on to a chopping board and position the
Swiss roll just above so that the left-hand side aligns with the
first teacake. Cut the Swiss roll at an angle on the right-hand
side, just behind the last teacake, for the boot heel. Put the
trimming at right angles to the first piece to form the boot leg.

2 Shape the boot toe and put the trimming at the top of the
boot leg to add extra height to the skate. Transfer all of the
cakes to the cake board or plate. Spread the cut edges of
the Swiss roll with jam.

3 Spread the fudge icing over the top and sides of the Swiss
roll and smooth with a knife.

4 Knead the yellow icing on a surface lightly dusted with icing
sugar until slightly softened. Roll out and cut a strip 18 x
10 cm (7 x 4 inches). Press on to the inside top of the boot
leg for a lining tongue. Knead and roll out the black icing,
cut a strip and press next to the yellow for the boot lining.

5 Knead and roll out two thirds of the grey icing and cut out a
curved shape for the boot leg reinforcement. Drape over the
boot leg and smooth in place. Cut a strip 12 x 1.5 cm (5 x
¾ inch), mark with knife cuts, then press on to the boot leg for
an adjustable strap. Make a small black clip with grey detail.

6 Roll out the remaining grey icing, cut a strip 20 x 5 cm
(8 x 2 inches) and shape to make a wheel guard. Press
halfway over the wheels and halfway over the boot base.

7 Cut 2 more strips for boot straps from the grey trimmings,
press in place and add clips as in Step 5. Roll out the
remaining black icing thinly, cut thin strips and squares and
press on to the boot for moulding detail. Roll small balls of
yellow and grey, flatten and stick to the wheels and leg
reinforcement with water for rivets.

Crashed skier

serves 8
decoration time 50 minutes, plus drying

50 g (2 oz) grey ready-to-roll icing

sifted icing sugar, for dusting

75 g (3 oz) black ready-to-roll icing

cocktail sticks

50 g (2 oz) red ready-to-roll icing

15 g (½ oz) pale pink ready-to-roll icing

1.2 litre (2 pint) pudding basin Small Madeira
     Cake (see page 12)

double quantity Butter Icing (see page 21)

20 cm (8 inch) thin square cake board or plate

4 tablespoons desiccated coconut

little black paste food colouring

Tips

- Remove the body and cocktail sticks before slicing the cake.
- If you are very short of time, use a washed child's action doll, cut the cake vertically in half and sandwich back together with the doll in the middle, or if using a broken doll, leave the cake whole. Put the clothes back on the doll once the cake has been iced.

1 Roll out the grey icing thickly and cut 2 skis 12 x 1 cm (5 x ½ inch). Round one end of each ski and curl up slightly. Shape 2 thin ropes 10 cm (4 inches) long for poles, taper one end of each, then wrap a thin rope around a little way from the tapered end. Leave to harden on a baking sheet lined with nonstick baking paper for 3 hours, or overnight.

2 Roll out the black icing thickly and cut 2 trouser legs 7 x 1 cm (3 x ½ inch). Stick a cocktail stick into one end of each so that it extends about 2.5 cm (1 inch). Stick grey ski boots to the other end with water. Leave to partially dry with the skis. Reserve the trimmings.

3 For the skier's arms and trunk, shape most of the red icing into a semicircle with a 6 cm (2½ inch) long base. Cut 2 cuts up from the base 1 cm (½ inch) in from either side but not all the way through and shape into outstretched arms. Shape the pink icing into a head with a small nose, adding a tiny skewer hole for the mouth. Add a black hat with red icing detail and attach to the shoulders with a cocktail stick. Shape a black scarf and gloves and add to the skier. Add 2 more cocktail sticks to the waist. Leave to dry.

4 Level the cake top, if needed. Cut horizontally in half and sandwich back together with a little butter icing. Put the cake, trimmed top downwards, on to the cake board or plate.

5 Reserve 1 tablespoon of the butter icing and spread the remainder over the top and side of the cake, and a little over the board or plate.

6 Press the body into the top of the cake and the legs halfway down. Spread a little butter icing over the trousers and body. Sprinkle the cake and skier with coconut. Attach skis to ski boots and poles to gloves. Paint on eyes with black colouring.

Chocolate extravaganza

serves 20
decoration time 30 minutes, plus drying

20 cm (8 inch) deep square chocolate-
  flavoured Large Madeira Cake
    (see page 13)

single quantity Glossy Chocolate Butter Icing
  (see page 22)

25 cm (10 inch) thick square cake board
  or plate

165 g (5½ oz) bag white chocolate-covered
  malt balls

165 g (5½ oz) bag milk chocolate-covered
  malt balls

1 Level the top of the cake, if needed. Cut the cake horizontally
   in half and sandwich back together with a little of the icing.

2 Put the cake on a wire rack set over a baking sheet and pour
   the remaining icing on to the cake top. Gently spread over
   the top and down the sides with a small palette knife,
   scooping up the icing from the baking sheet to fill in any
   gaps at the base of the cake.

3 Carefully transfer the cake to the cake board or plate.
   Arrange alternate-coloured malt balls in diagonal rows over
   the top of the cake, with a single row around the base of the
   cake. Leave to set in a cool place for at least 30 minutes
   before serving.

Tip

Vary the sweets on top of the cake
according to your child's preference or
make the cake multicoloured by adding
a variety of sweets in different colours.

Hearts and flowers

serves 14–16
decoration time 30 minutes

1 Put the cake on to a chopping board and level the top, if needed. Make a greaseproof paper heart template by drawing around the cake board and cutting out the heart. Trim a little off all the way around the template edge until it fits the cake top. Cut the cake around the heart template.

2 Cut the cake horizontally in half and sandwich back together with some of the butter icing. Transfer to the cake board. Spread the remaining butter icing over the top and side of the cake.

3 Lightly knead the pale pink icing on a surface lightly dusted with icing sugar until slightly softened. Roll out until a little larger than the cake. Lift on a rolling pin and drape over the cake, then smooth in place with your fingertips dusted with icing sugar. Trim off the excess.

4 Re-knead the trimmings and roll out. Cut out flower and heart shapes of different sizes using plunger cutters, pressing them out on to a piece of foam sponge so that they curl (see page 32), then transfer to a baking sheet lined with nonstick baking paper dusted with a little icing sugar. Make dark pink or red and white flowers and hearts in the same way from the remaining ready-to-roll icing.

5 Arrange the flowers and hearts over the cake top and stick in place with tiny dots of piping icing or piped royal icing. Add dots of icing to the centre of some of the larger flowers and add candles. Tie the ribbon around the side of the cake and decorate the cake board with extra flowers and hearts.

23 cm (9 inch) deep round Large Madeira Cake (see page 13)

24 cm (9½ inch) thin heart-shaped cake board

one-and-a-half quantity Butter Icing (see page 21)

625 g (1¼ lb) pale pink ready-to-roll icing

sifted icing sugar, for dusting

75 g (3 oz) deep pink or red ready-to-roll icing

75 g (3 oz) white ready-to-roll icing

1 tube white piping icing or 2 tablespoons Royal Icing (see page 25)

pale pink candles

1 metre (39 inches) x 2.5 cm (1 inch) wide pink ribbon

Tip

For a St. Valentine's Day version, use a chocolate-flavoured cake and cover it with a single quantity of Glossy Chocolate Butter Icing (see page 22) and add red and pink hearts of varying size.

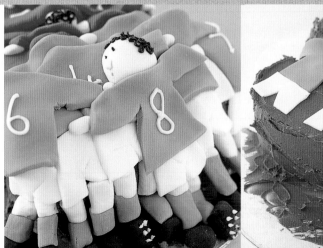

Rugby scrum

serves 14–16
decoration time 1¼ hours

1 Level the top of the cake, if needed. Trim off and round the corners to make an hour-glass shape, then slope the opposite sides of the cake slightly for the players to lean against.

2 Cut the cake horizontally in half and sandwich back together with butter icing. Put the cake on to the cake board or plate. Spread butter icing thinly over the top and sides and roughly on the board or plate to resemble a muddy pitch.

3 Knead the green (or favourite team's colour) icing on a surface lightly dusted with icing sugar until slightly softened. Divide into 10 pieces. Reserve 2 pieces for socks and roll each of the remaining pieces into a 6 cm (2½ inch) square. Make a small cut on either side of each square in from the bottom corner and almost to the top of the square, then shape into arms and a body. Arrange one row of 3 shirts facing the centre of the cake, with arms stretched over the next player's shoulders. Knead and roll out the white icing and add a row of rectangular white shorts with a small slit in the base of each. Add a second row of 4 shirts and shorts a little back from the first, with the shirts curving over the edge of the cake. Add the eighth man to the centre of the side of the cake. Repeat for the team on the other side of the scrum.

4 Knead the pink icing and shape a head for each player on the edge of the scrum and one or two extra heads with button noses and small holes for mouths. Shape hands for the players.

5 Shape short pink sausage shapes for thighs and same-sized pieces from the teams' coloured icing reserved in Step 3 for socks. Add black oval pieces for boots. Shape a rugby ball from the remaining black icing and trim with white icing.

6 Pipe on black hair and facial features. Pipe white numbers on to the shirt backs and studs on some boots.

20 cm (8 inch) deep square chocolate-flavoured Large Madeira Cake (see page 13)

one-and-a-half quantity chocolate-flavoured Butter Icing (see page 21)

33 cm (13 inch) thin round cake board or plate

375 g (12 oz) green ready-to-roll icing (or favourite team's colour)

sifted icing sugar, for dusting

375 g (12 oz) red ready-to-roll icing (or opponent team's colour)

250 g (8 oz) white ready-to-roll icing

250 g (8 oz) pink ready-to-roll icing

150 g (5 oz) black ready-to-roll icing

1 tablespoon Royal Icing (see page 25), coloured black, or 1 tube black writing icing

2 tablespoons white Royal Icing (see page 25) or 1 tube white writing icing

Tip

Modify the shirts, socks and numbers to adapt this cake for American football and create ready-to-roll icing helmets and shoulder pads for the players. Choose colours to match your favourite teams.

Funky boots

serves 10
decoration time 1 hour, plus drying

2 x 28 cm (11 inch) chocolate-flavoured Swiss Rolls (see page 18) or 2 x 28 cm (11 inch) bought chocolate Swiss rolls

3 tablespoons raspberry jam

4–6 long wooden satay sticks

500 g (1 lb) mauve ready-to-roll icing

sifted icing sugar, for dusting

18 cm (7 inch) square cake board or plate

125 g (4 oz) pale pink ready-to-roll icing

200 g (7 oz) deep pink ready-to-roll icing

Tips

• If the boots seem a little wobbly, stand a tall sauce bottle or bag of flour behind each boot leg before leaving to dry. The boots are best iced the day before they are needed.

• Make sure you remove the satay sticks before serving the cake to guests.

1 Cut each Swiss roll in half. Put two Swiss roll halves a little apart on a chopping board for the boot feet. Stand a second half of Swiss roll on top of one at one end for the boot leg and secure with jam and satay sticks. Repeat to make a second boot leg. Shape the boot feet by trimming away a little of the cake.

2 Spread the cakes thinly with the remaining jam. Cut the mauve icing in half, wrap one half and reserve. Knead the remaining half on a surface lightly dusted with icing sugar until slightly softened. Roll out thinly and drape over one of the boots so that any joins will fall on the inside face of the boot. Smooth in place with your fingertips dusted with icing sugar. Trim off the excess. Fill any gaps with trimmings. Cover the second boot in the same way. Carefully transfer to the cake board or plate.

3 Knead and roll out the pale pink icing. Cut out two 6 cm (2½ inch) rounds with a plain biscuit cutter and press on to the top of the boot legs. Reserve the trimmings.

4 Knead and roll out the deep pink icing. Cut long strips 1 cm (½ inch) wide. Press one around the top of each boot and a second around the base of each boot, sticking in place with a little water, and trim off the excess.

5 Cut heart shapes from re-rolled icing trimmings using 3 different-sized small cutters, then cut smaller shapes from the 2 larger ones. Stick in place with water. Leave for at least 1 hour for the icing to harden.

Handbag heaven

serves 14–16
decoration time 50 minutes

20 cm (8 inch) deep square Large Madeira
    Cake (see page 13)

one-and-a-half quantity Butter Icing
    (see page 21)

36 x 25 cm (14 x 10 inch) rectangular cake
    board or large plate

750 g (1½ lb) pale pink ready-to-roll icing

sifted icing sugar, for dusting

150 g (5 oz) white ready-to-roll icing

250 g (8 oz) pale green ready-to-roll icing

6 pink sugar flowers

Tip

For an adult version, use a favourite
handbag as a guide and copy colours,
clasp and handle detail.

1 Put the cake on to a chopping board and level the top, if needed. Cut a thin curved slice from the top 2 opposite sides of the cake to about one-third down the length of the cake. To do so, turn the first piece of trimmed cake over and use it as a template to cut the second side. Slope the top edge of the handbag down towards the narrow side so that the edge where the handbag flap will go is shallower.

2 Cut the cake horizontally in half and sandwich back together with two-thirds of the butter icing. Put on to the cake board or plate. Reserve 2 teaspoons of the butter icing and spread the remainder thinly over the top and sides of the cake.

3 Knead the pink icing on a surface lightly dusted with icing sugar until slightly softened. Roll out thinly and use to cover the cake, smoothing with your fingertips dusted with icing sugar. Trim off the excess, wrap and reserve.

4 Knead the white icing, roll out thickly and cut out the top flap of the handbag. Press in place, smoothing with your fingertips. Reserve the trimmings.

5 Knead and roll out the pale green icing. Cut long strips 1 cm (½ inch) wide and stick as stripes on to the lower part of the bag with water, butting up against the flap and leaving space in between so the pink icing can be seen. Trim off the excess.

6 Cut a rectangle of pink icing 4 x 1 cm (1½ x ½ inch) and press on to the flap for a clasp. Cut a smaller green rectangle and add at right angles to the pink. Cut a white strip for a buckle. Stick flowers on to the flap with the reserved butter icing.

7 Roll the remaining pink, white and green icing into small balls and arrange alternate colours as a strap on the cake board, butting up to the handbag top.

Chocolate bliss

serves 6
decoration time 45 minutes, plus drying

Shallow Cake (see page 17)

single quantity vanilla-flavoured Butter Icing
(see page 21)

25 cm (10 inch) round cake board, covered
with 200 g (7 oz) deep pink ready-to-roll
icing, or plate

900 ml (1½ pint) pudding basin Medium
Madeira Cake, made with half the 4-egg
mixture (see page 13)

625 g (1¼ lb) turquoise-blue ready-to-roll icing

sifted icing sugar, for dusting

cocktail sticks

40 g (1½ oz) milk or plain dark chocolate

1–2 teaspoons milk

few large marshmallows

100 g (3½ oz) bag candy-covered chocolate
drops

2 tablespoons Royal Icing (see page 25) or
1 tube writing icing

Tips

- Make sure you remove the cocktail sticks
  before serving the cake to guests.
- Coloured spots, hearts or flowers could
  be cut from coloured ready-to-roll icing
  as an alternative to the sweets spots on
  the cup and saucer.

1 Spread the top and sides of the shallow cake thinly with
butter icing and put on a chopping board. Level the basin
cake top, if needed, then place, trimmed top downwards,
on to a chopping board. Cut horizontally in half and
sandwich back together with some of the butter icing.
Spread a little more of the butter icing thinly over the outside
of the basin cake.

2 Knead the turquoise-blue icing on a surface lightly dusted
with icing sugar until slightly softened. Cut off 150 g (5 oz)
and wrap and reserve the remainder. Roll out the measured
icing and use to cover the shallow cake, smoothing the
surface with your fingertips dusted with icing sugar. Trim off
the excess. Transfer to the cake board or plate.

3 Roll out the remaining blue icing and drape over the basin
cake. Smooth over the surface, then carefully turn up the
other way to resemble a cup. Trim off the excess and smooth
the top edge. Put on to the shallow cake.

4 Re-knead the trimmings, roll into a thick rope 12 x 1 cm
(5 x ½ inch) and shape into a cup handle. Press on to the
cup side and secure with cocktail sticks. Prop up with pieces
of crumpled foil.

5 Put the chocolate in a heatproof bowl and melt over a
saucepan half-filled with gently simmering water. Stir into
the remaining butter icing, mixing in enough milk to make
a smooth glossy icing. Spread over the top of the cup and
add the marshmallows to the centre.

6 Stick the coloured sweets over the cup and saucer with
piped dots of royal or writing icing. Leave to harden for at
least 1 hour. Remove the foil from under the cup handle
before serving.

white chocolate treats

serves 8
decoration time 45 minutes, plus chilling

1 Trim the top of the cake level then, using a 6 cm (2½ inch) plain biscuit cutter or upturned tumbler as a template, cut out 8 smaller rounds of cake from the large cake using a small serrated knife. Cut each cake horizontally in half.

2 Add a spoonful of the white chocolate cream to 8 cake halves, then top with the remaining cake halves. Spread some white chocolate cream thickly over the top of each cake and then thinly around the sides.

3 Put the white chocolate in a heatproof bowl set over a saucepan half-filled with just-boiled water. Set aside for 5 minutes or so, off the heat, until the chocolate has melted. Cut 8 strips of nonstick baking paper 20 x 8.5 cm (8 x 3½ inches). Stir the chocolate, then spread over one strip right up to one long edge and then make a wavy swirled edge a little way down from the opposite long edge. With the wavy edge uppermost, press the strip of paper so that the chocolate touches the cream-spread edge of the cake and stands a little above the top. Smooth in place and repeat until all the cakes have been wrapped in the same way. Chill for 2 hours or until set.

4 Carefully peel the paper away from the chocolate, top the cakes with foil-wrapped sweets and decorate the sides of the cakes with ribbon. Transfer to a plate or cake board. Chill in the refrigerator until ready to serve.

23 cm (9 inch) deep round Large Madeira Cake (see page 13)

single quantity White Chocolate Cream (see page 24)

250 g (8 oz) white chocolate, broken into pieces

400 g (13 oz) foil-wrapped sweets

selection of thick and thin jewel-coloured ribbons in 3 colours, such as purple, pale pink and cerise pink

large round or square plate or cake board

Tips

- A plain dark chocolate version could be created in the same way, with small strawberries added to the tops of the cakes instead of the sweets.
- The cake trimmings may be used for a trifle or could be eaten as a cook's perk!

Flowers and butterflies

serves 8
decoration time 1 hour, plus chilling/drying

50 g (2 oz) white chocolate, broken into pieces

50 g (2 oz) plain dark chocolate

125 g (4 oz) pale pink ready-to-roll icing

sifted icing sugar, for dusting

18 cm (7 inch) deep round chocolate-flavoured
    Small Madeira Cake (see page 12)

single quantity Double Chocolate Ganache
    (see page 23)

23 cm (9 inch) pale pink cake board or plate

Tip

If the butterflies seem a little soft when you
take them out of the refrigerator, freeze
them for 10 minutes. You may find it helpful
to prop up the wings with some of the tiny
pink flowers.

1 Put the white chocolate in a heatproof bowl set over a
saucepan half-filled with just-boiled water. Set aside for
5 minutes or so, off the heat, until the chocolate has melted.
Stir, then spoon into a nonstick baking paper piping bag and
snip off the tip (see page 31). Pipe pairs of butterfly wings, in
the shape of a capital 'B' with its mirrored reflection for the
other wing, on to a baking sheet lined with nonstick baking
paper. Fill in the centres with squiggly piped lines and pipe
separate bodies, if liked.

2 Melt the plain dark chocolate in a separate bowl and use to
pipe butterflies as before. Chill the decorations in the
refrigerator for 45 minutes or until firm.

3 Meanwhile, knead the pale pink icing on a surface lightly
dusted with icing sugar until slightly softened. Roll out and
stamp out flower shapes with 4 different-sized biscuit cutters
ranging from 3 to 7 cm (1¼ to 3 inches) and some tiny
flowers with plunger cutters. Curl the petals by pressing into
sections of a bun tray lined with crumpled nonstick baking
paper (see page 32). Leave to dry for 30 minutes.

4 Cut the cake horizontally in half and sandwich back together
with some of the ganache. Transfer to the plate or cake
board. Reserve 1 tablespoon of the ganache and spread the
remainder over the top and side of the cake, smoothing with
a small palette knife.

5 Arrange the flowers over the top of the cake, with a few
around the base of the cake. Carefully lift the butterfly wings
off the paper and arrange in the flowers with dots of piped
ganache, then add the bodies to the butterflies, if using. Add
pale pink flower candles in between the flower and butterfly
icing decorations, if liked.

Bowled over

serves 12
decoration time 45 minutes

30 x 23 x 5 cm (12 x 9 x 2 inch) roasting tin
    Medium Madeira Cake (see page 13)

one-and-a-half quantity Butter Icing
    (see page 21)

33 x 25 cm (13 x 10 inch) rectangular cake
    board, covered with 375 g (12 oz) royal
    blue ready-to-roll icing, or plate

750 g (1½ lb) white ready-to-roll icing

sifted icing sugar, for dusting

200 g (7 oz) black ready-to-roll icing

75 g (3 oz) orange ready-to-roll icing

50 g (2 oz) turquoise ready-to-roll icing

Tip

If your child is a member of a bowling
club, then match the markings on the
skittles with those at the bowling alley.

1 Put the roasting tin cake on a chopping board so that the
short edges are facing you. Cut a little off the top left- and
right-hand sides to resemble the necks of 3 skittles, standing
close together. Shape the bottom short edge into 3 curves
for the skittle bases.

2 Cut the trimmed cake horizontally in half and sandwich back
together with some butter icing. Put on to the cake board or
plate and spread the top and sides thinly with the butter icing.

3 Cut off 250 g (8 oz) of the white icing, wrap and reserve.
Knead the remaining icing on a surface lightly dusted with
icing sugar until slightly softened. Roll out and use to cover
the cake, smoothing in place with your fingertips dusted with
icing sugar. Trim off the excess.

4 Re-knead one-third of the icing trimmings, roll out and cut into
a tall skittle shape, the height of the cake and about one-third
the width. Press on to the left-hand side of the cake top.

5 Knead and roll out the remaining white icing and cut out
2 more skittle shapes. Add one to the right-hand side of the
cake, then press the third in the centre.

6 Knead and roll out the black icing. Cut out thin strips and use
to edge the sides of the skittle markings and decorate the
top. Stick in place with a little water. Reserve the trimmings.

7 Knead and roll out the orange icing. Cut out small rectangles
and 3 narrow strips. Use to decorate the skittles. Knead and
roll out the turquoise icing and cut into a 10 cm (4 inch)
circle. Position on top of the skittles for the ball. Roll out the
reserved black trimmings, cut out a number for the age of the
birthday child, then press on to the ball.

Riding champ

serves 8–10
decoration time 1 hour

1 Level the cake top, if necessary. Turn the cake over, trimmed top downwards, cut into 3 horizontal layers and sandwich together with butter icing. Reserve 2 teaspoons of the butter icing and spread the remainder thinly over the top and side of the cake. Spread the reserved butter icing over half the cake board.

2 Knead the black icing on a surface lightly dusted with icing sugar until slightly softened. Cut off 50 g (2 oz) and wrap. Roll out the remainder until it covers half the cake board. Drape over the butter-iced end of the cake board for the hat peak and smooth with your fingertips dusted with icing sugar. Trim off the excess. Re-knead the trimmings and roll out. Cut out 2 ribbons for the back of the hat and 2 small buttons. Transfer to a sheet of nonstick baking paper.

3 Put the cake on to the cake board so that it almost touches the un-iced end and slightly covers the black 'hat peak' end.

4 Draw a triangular template for the coloured silks on nonstick baking paper with a base 11 cm (4½ inches) long and a height of 15 cm (6 inches). Cut out.

5 Knead the pale pink icing, roll out and use the template to cut out 3 triangular shapes. Press lightly on to the cake, leaving spaces in between. Cut out 3 deep pink triangles and press into the gaps, readjusting the position of the triangles slightly as necessary, trimming away the excess or pressing the edges together so that the cake is neatly covered. Smooth with your fingertips dusted with icing sugar.

6 Put the cake board on to a plate and place the black ribbons at the back. Roll out the reserved black icing and cut a strip 51 x 2 cm (21 x ¾ inches). Stick around the base of the hat with a little water. Add a black button to back and top.

1.5 litre (2½ pint) pudding basin Medium Madeira Cake (see page 13)

single quantity Butter Icing (see page 21)

23 x 18 cm (9 x 7 inch) thin oval cake board or plate

250 g (8 oz) black ready-to-roll icing

sifted icing sugar, for dusting

250 g (8 oz) pale pink ready-to-roll icing

250 g (8 oz) deep pink ready-to-roll icing

Tip
You may like to add a ribbon or icing rosette to finish off the cake, with the age of your child or a birthday message piped or written on to the centre. See page 74 for details of how to make a rosette from ready-to-roll icing.

Ice cream dream

serves 12
decoration time 50 minutes

30 x 23 x 5 cm (12 x 9 x 2 inch) roasting tin
chocolate-flavoured Medium Madeira Cake
(see page 13)

double quantity vanilla-flavoured Butter Icing
(see page 21)

35 x 25 cm (14 x 10 inch) rectangular cake
board, covered with 375 g (12 oz) lilac
ready-to-roll icing, or plate

500 g (1 lb) pale yellow ready-to-roll icing

4 chocolate-flavoured Muffins (see page 17)
or large bought muffins

pink or red paste food colouring

green paste food colouring

brown paste food colouring

1 To make the cone, cut the roasting tin cake into a triangle 18 x 23 cm (7 x 9 inches) on a chopping board. The trimmings are not needed (see Tip).

2 Cut the cone horizontally in half and sandwich back together with some butter icing. Spread the top and sides thinly with butter icing. Transfer the cone to the cake board or plate.

3 Knead the yellow ready-to-roll icing on a surface lightly dusted with icing sugar until slightly softened. Roll out two thirds, drape over the cone to completely cover and smooth in place. Trim off the excess and knead with the remaining icing. Roll out and use to cover the left half of the cone. Smooth in place and trim off the excess. Mark the icing with criss-cross lines to resemble wafer biscuit.

4 Trim a vertical slice off 2 of the muffins, then butt against the cone, with a third muffin above them. Trim a slice off the base of the remaining muffin and set aside.

5 Divide the butter icing into four portions, leaving one plain. Colour the second pink, the third pale green and the remaining portion light brown. Spread each colour over a different muffin and arrange as ice cream scoops, with the trimmed edges butted next to the cone.

Tip

To make use of the cake trimmings, split and sandwich them together with extra butter icing, spreading some on top too. Cut into small shapes and decorate with sweets. Alternatively, use the sponge as the base for a trifle or tiramisu.

Gifts galore

serves 28
decoration time 1¼ hours

1. Level the cake tops, if needed. Cut each cake horizontally in half and sandwich back together with butter icing. Put the square cake on to the cake board and spread the top and sides thinly with a little butter icing. Reserve 1 tablespoon of the butter icing and spread the remainder over the other 2 cakes. Put these cakes aside.

2. Cut off one-quarter of the burgundy icing, wrap and reserve. Knead the remaining icing on a surface lightly dusted with icing sugar until slightly softened. Roll out and use to cover the square cake, smoothing in place with your fingertips dusted with icing sugar. Trim off the excess and reserve.

3. Cut off one-third of the white icing, wrap and reserve. Use the remainder to cover the larger round cake. Trim off the excess and reserve. Put on top of the square cake.

4. Cut off one-quarter of the blue icing, wrap and reserve. Use the remainder to cover the small round cake. Trim off the excess and reserve. Put on top of the other cakes.

5. Roll out the reserved blue icing and cut 4 strips 9 x 2.5 cm (3½ x 1 inch). Stick to the sides of the base cake with butter icing, to resemble ribbons. Trim the tops of the strips where they butt up against the round cake. Reserve the trimmings.

6. Make burgundy ribbon strips for the centre cake and white strips for the top cake in the same way. Cut an extra strip of white and form into 2 loops for a bow, adding 2 smaller strips for the ribbon ends.

7. Roll out the remaining blue icing trimmings and cut tiny rounds with the upturned end of a piping tube. Stick over the centre cake with a little water. Cover the top of the cake board with a strip of white icing (see page 29). Stick the ribbon on to the side of the cake board with sticky tape.

20 cm (8 inch) deep square Large Madeira Cake (see page 13)

1 x Small Madeira Cake mixture (see page 12) split between 1 x 15 cm (6 inch) deep round tin and 1 x 9 cm (3½ inch) small baked bean can (see Tips), baked

double quantity Butter Icing (see page 21)

25 cm (10 inch) thick square cake board

750 g (1½ lb) burgundy ready-to-roll icing

sifted icing sugar, for dusting

500 g (1 lb) white ready-to-roll icing

250 g (8 oz) pale blue ready-to-roll icing

1 metre (39 inches) x 1 cm (½ inch) narrow white ribbon

double-sided sticky tape

Tips
- Use a 200 g (7 oz) baked bean can for the tiny cake.
- Remove the top and bottom of the baked bean can before use, wash well and peel away the label. Stand it on a baking sheet and line with nonstick or greaseproof paper as if lining the base and sides of a larger tin (see page 11).

Animal
magic

My little kitten

serves 10
decoration time 30 minutes

2 small sandwich cakes (see page 15), each
    filled with 2 tablespoons jam, or 2 bought
    filled vanilla or chocolate sandwich cakes

30 x 25 cm (12 x 10 inch) oval cake board or
    large plate

double quantity Butter Icing (see page 21)

red and yellow or orange food colouring

2 jumbo green candy-coated chocolate beans

2 standard brown candy-coated chocolate
    beans

6 chocolate sticks

125 g (4 oz) orange ready-to-roll icing

sifted icing sugar, for dusting

1 Put one cake on to the cake board or plate for the body then
prop the second up against it for the cat's head.

2 Spoon one third of the butter icing into a separate bowl and
colour it orange.

3 Spread the head and body with the remaining uncoloured
butter icing, then spoon on some orange butter icing to
create the effect of ginger markings, easing it into stripes and
swirls with the tip of a small knife.

4 Press the green sweetie eyes in position, then stick on brown
sweetie eyeballs with a little butter icing. Break a little off the
end of the chocolate sticks and press into the cake for
whiskers. Knead the orange ready-to-roll icing on a surface
dusted with a little icing sugar. Shape a small ball into a
nose shape, then use more icing to create two triangular
ears, four round paws and a thin rope for the mouth. Mark
the paws with a knife and add to the cake.

Tip

If the cake is very crumbly, spread it with a
little jam before topping with the butter
icing so that the crumbs are stuck in place.

Puppy love

serves 10
decoration time 1 hour, plus drying

1.2 litre (2 pint) and 750 ml (1¼ pint)
   pudding basin Medium Madeira Cakes
   (see page 13)

25 cm (10 inch) thin round cake board or plate

double quantity vanilla-flavoured Butter Icing
   (see page 21)

cocktail sticks

4 bought mini jam sponge rolls

200 g (7oz) bar white chocolate

15 g (½ oz) white ready-to-roll icing

sifted icing sugar, for dusting

40 g (1½ oz) black ready-to-roll icing

15 g (½ oz) red ready-to-roll icing

125 g (4 oz) pale yellow ready-to-roll icing

Tip
Make sure you remove the cocktail sticks
before serving the cake to guests.

1 Level the basin cake tops, if necessary. Put the larger one, trimmed top downwards, on to the cake board or plate for the dog's body. Spread the outside with a little butter icing. Put the smaller cake on top, trimmed top downwards, slightly off centre for the head, and secure with butter icing and cocktail sticks.

2 Scoop out eye sockets in the top cake with a teaspoon and shape a small muzzle. Stick 2 sponge roll front legs at the front of the cake with a little butter icing and the remaining 2 towards the back for back legs.

3 Reserve 3 teaspoons of the butter icing and spread the remainder all over the cake to cover completely.

4 Run a swivel-bladed vegetable peeler over the smooth underside of the chocolate bar to create curls (see page 32). Stick the curls all over the dog with a round-bladed knife.

5 Roll small balls of white icing for the eyes, flatten into ovals and press in place. Add tiny balls of black icing for eyeballs and stick in place with dots of butter icing. Shape the remaining black icing into a round nose and stick on to the muzzle. Mark with the end of a cocktail stick. Shape the red icing into a curved tongue and add to the face.

6 Roll out two-thirds of the yellow icing thickly and cut out floppy ears. Stick in place with a little of the reserved butter icing, propping them up with pieces of crumpled foil or nonstick baking paper. Roll a ball of yellow icing, cut in half and make 3 small cuts in each half. Add to the front legs for paws. Shape 2 larger back paws from short sausage shapes and add cuts as before. Shape the remaining icing into a tail and press in place. Leave for at least 30 minutes for the ears to harden, then remove the foil or paper before serving.

Cute teddy

serves 8
decoration time 45 minutes, plus drying

900 ml (1½ pint) pudding basin chocolate-
  flavoured Medium Madeira Cake, made
  with half the 4-egg mixture (see page 13)

25 x 20 cm (10 x 8 inch) oval cake board
  or plate

cocktail sticks

1 large chocolate Muffin (see page 17), or a
  large bought muffin, paper case removed

2 bought mini chocolate sponge rolls

2 bought sponge finger biscuits

single quantity Chocolate Fudge Icing (see
  page 22)

100 g (3½ oz) pale blue ready-to-roll icing

sifted icing sugar, for dusting

2 foil-wrapped chocolate coins, unwrapped, or
  2 jumbo chocolate buttons

15 g (½ oz) white ready-to-roll icing

2 blue mini candy-covered chocolate drops

1 brown candy-covered chocolate drop

pink paste food colouring

2 sugar flowers

50 cm (20 inch) fine ribbon (optional)

Tip

Make sure you remove the ribbon and
cocktail sticks before serving the cake to
birthday guests.

1 Level the basin cake top, if necessary. Put it, trimmed top downwards, on to the cake board or plate. Press 3 cocktail sticks into the domed top of the cake, then press the muffin on to the sticks so that the rounded top is facing forwards for the bear's head. Add the mini sponge rolls for the legs and sponge finger biscuits for the arms, attaching to the cake with more cocktail sticks.

2 Reserve 2 teaspoons of the fudge icing. Spread the remainder over the cake and rough up with the back of the knife so that it resembles fur. Leave for a few minutes to harden slightly.

3 Knead the blue icing on a surface lightly dusted with icing sugar until slightly softened. Roll out and cut out a waistcoat shape. Press on to the bear, adjusting the shape of the waistcoat, if necessary, with scissors.

4 Re-knead the trimmings. Roll small balls for the paws, flatten, then press on to the ends of the arms and legs. Add tiny flattened balls to the feet for claws.

5 To make the ears, press a small flattened ball of blue icing on to each chocolate coin or button, then press into the top of the head. Shape tiny flattened ovals of white icing for eyes and add mini candy-covered chocolate drops for eyeballs, sticking in place with dots of the reserved fudge icing. Add the brown candy-covered chocolate drop for the nose. Colour the remaining white icing pink, roll out and cut out a mouth shape. Press on to the bear's face. Add the sugar flowers for buttons, sticking in place with dots of fudge icing. Complete with a ribbon around the neck, if liked.

Mini duck ponds

makes 12
decoration time 30 minutes

12 Fairy Cakes (see page 16), or bought
   fairy cakes

single quantity Glacé Icing (see page 24)

blue paste food colouring

3 tablespoons desiccated coconut

green paste food colouring

300 g (10 oz) yellow ready-to-roll icing

sifted icing sugar, for dusting

25 g (1 oz) orange ready-to-roll icing

2 tablespoons Royal Icing (see page 25),
   coloured green, or 1 tube green
   writing icing

25 cm (10 inch) round cake board or plate

1 Level the cake tops, if necessary. Colour the glacé icing blue with the colouring, then spoon on to the cake tops and smooth with the back of the spoon.

2 Put the coconut in a small bowl with a little of the green colouring and mix with a spoon until pale green. Sprinkle around the edges of the blue icing 'ponds'.

3 Knead the yellow icing on a surface lightly dusted with icing sugar until slightly softened. Tear off small pieces and make 12 oval-shaped duck bodies 2.5 cm (1 inch) long and 12 small oval heads 2 cm (¾ inch) long. Press the heads on to the bodies and stick in place with a little water, if necessary.

4 Re-knead the trimmings, roll out and cut out six 5 cm (2 inch) rounds with a fluted biscuit cutter. Cut each round into quarters, then stick a pair of quarters on each duck as wings, with the fluted edge as the wing tips, using a little water.

5 Knead and roll out the orange icing. Shape tiny triangular beaks and stick on to the ducks with a little water. Sit the ducks on the mini ponds and use royal or writing icing to pipe on green eyes. Transfer to the cake board or plate.

Tip

As an alternative, Easter-themed, design, you could make smaller wings and transform the ducks into chickens, then sit them on nests of crumbled chocolate flake with mini chocolate eggs in the centre.

My first pony

serves 8–10
decoration time 45 minutes

1 Draw a horse's head on a piece of paper the same size as the cake. Cut it out and use as a template to cut the shape from the cake. Cut two triangular ears from the trimmings.

2 Cut the cake horizontally in half and sandwich back together with some of the butter icing. Spread the remaining butter icing thinly over the top and sides of the cake, adding the ears and covering them with butter icing. Transfer to the cake board or plate.

3 Knead the brown icing on a surface lightly dusted with icing sugar until slightly softened. Roll out the icing and use to cover the cake. Smooth in place with your fingertips dusted with icing sugar. Trim off the excess. Re-knead and wrap the trimmings. Mark a mouth with the handle of a small brush.

4 Knead and roll out the black icing. Cut strips for bridle and reins and place on the cake, sticking in position with a little water. Cut a circle of icing with an upturned piping nozzle then cut out a smaller circle with another piping tube. Position where the reins meet the bridle at the mouth.

5 Roll out a little of the brown trimmings, and cut out 2 brown ears and an eye socket. Press on to the cake, adding a black eyeball. Knead extra brown colouring into the remaining brown icing to darken. Re-roll the dark brown and black trimmings and cut petal shapes for the mane. Stick on to the neck with water. Add a red rosette (see page 74), if liked. Pipe your child's name or age on to the rosette, if liked.

30 x 23 x 5 cm (12 x 9 x 2 inch) roasting tin chocolate-flavoured Medium Madeira Cake (see page 13)

one-and-a-half quantity Butter Icing (see page 21)

38 x 33 cm (15 x 13 inch) oval cake board, covered with 500 g (1 lb) pale green ready-to-roll icing, or a plate

500 g (1 lb) brown ready-to-roll icing

sifted icing sugar, for dusting

150 g (5 oz) black ready-to-roll icing

brown paste food colouring

125 g (4 oz) red ready-to-roll icing (optional)

Tip

For a child who is regularly taking riding lessons, adapt the colouring to suit their favourite pony at the stables.

Scary shark

serves 12
decoration time 1 hour

30 x 23 x 5 cm (12 x 9 x 2 inch) roasting tin
   Medium Madeira Cake (see page 13)

28 x 23 cm (11 x 9 inch) thin oval cake board

one-and-a-half quantity Butter Icing
   (see page 21), coloured red

500 g (1 lb) black ready-to-roll icing

sifted icing sugar, for dusting

125 g (4 oz) white ready-to-roll icing

2 yellow and black liquorice sweets

black paper

35 x 30 cm (14 x 12 inch) cake board or plate

Tip

Use black paste food colouring for a really
dark colour or buy ready-coloured black
icing from specialist cake-icing shops.

1   Put the cake on to a chopping board so the top is uppermost and the short sides are facing you. Measure 12 cm (5 inches) up from the bottom left-hand corner, repeat on the other side and 19 cm (7½ inches) up in the centre then cut between the marks in an arched line. Set aside for the shark's head. Cut a 10 cm (4 inch) deep semicircle from the remaining cake, using the uncut edge as the base, for the jaw. Discard the trimmings.

2   Put the jaw on to the cake board with the curved edge almost touching one end. Graduate the straight edge of the back of the jaw so the other cake section will sit comfortably, then place the shark's head on top, half on the jaw, half off, to make the mouth. Fill in the gaps underneath the top cake with trimmings.

3   Spread the mouth area of the cakes thickly with butter icing, then spread the rest thinly over the top and sides of the cake.

4   Knead and roll out one-third of the black icing to a long strip and trim to 37.5 x 5 cm (15 x 2 inches). Carefully lift and press around the jaw base and a little over the head base, smoothing in place with your fingertips. Roll out the remaining icing, curve one edge and press the curved edge up to the curved edge on top of the shark's head. Drape over the sides, down to the back of the cake board, and smooth in place. Trim off the excess icing and reserve.

5   Cut triangles for teeth from the thinly rolled white icing. Press the top teeth in place first, then the bottom teeth. Add 2 liquorice sweet eyeballs. Shape 2 black eyelids and press over the eyeballs. Cut 3 fins 18 cm (7 inches) long and a tail 43 cm (17 inches) long from black paper. Fold along the base of one fin and stand on the cake top. Put the other 2 fins and tail on the large cake board or plate, place the shark cake on top then curl the end of the tail so that it stands up.

Timid tortoise

serves 8
decoration time 1 hour

1 Level the cake top, if necessary. Put, trimmed top downwards, on to a chopping board, cut horizontally in half and sandwich back together with some of the butter icing. Spread a little butter icing thinly all over the top and side of the cake then put it on to the cake board or plate.

2 Make a hexagon paper template by cutting a circle of paper 4 cm (1¾ inches) in diameter. (The top of a spice jar is an ideal size for this.) Fold in half then into three to make six segments. Cut a straight line from each tip of the fold to the other then open out.

3 Cut off one-quarter of the yellow icing, wrap and reserve. Knead the remaining yellow icing on a surface lightly dusted with icing sugar until slightly softened. Roll out thinly. Repeat with the pink and blue icing.

4 Cut out several hexagons. Put one yellow hexagon in the centre of the cake then arrange alternate-coloured shapes in 3 rings around the tortoise's shell, rolling and cutting the icing trimmings until the tortoise is completely covered.

5 Knead the remaining pink icing and shape four small legs and a head. Butt up against the cake. Knead and roll out the reserved yellow icing, shape into a long rope, then flatten with a rolling pin and trim to 62 cm (25 inches) long by 1 cm (½ inch) wide. Press around the base of the tortoise's shell. Shape the tortoise's eyes and eyelids from blue and pink icing and stick on to the cake with water. Make a mouth with a cocktail stick.

6 Decorate the cake board with sugar flowers, cut with different-sized plunger cutters (see page 32), if liked.

20 cm (8 inch) mixing bowl Small Madeira Cake (see page 12)

one-and-a-half quantity Butter Icing (see page 21)

28 cm (11 inch) thin round cake board, covered with 375 g (12 oz) pale green icing, or plate

375 g (12 oz) pale yellow ready-to-roll icing

sifted icing sugar, for dusting

375 g (12 oz) pale pink ready-to-roll icing

150 g (5 oz) pale blue ready-to-roll icing

few sugar flowers (optional)

Tip

You may find it easier to roll out small pieces of coloured icing with a child's rolling pin, making just enough hexagons for one ring at a time so that they don't dry out as you stick them on.

Fearless lion

serves 14–16
decoration time 30 minutes

23 cm (9 inch) deep round Large Madeira
Cake (see page 13)

1 bought mini sponge roll

25 cm (10 inch) thin round cake board or plate

double quantity Butter Icing (see page 21)

yellow paste food colouring

red paste food colouring

black paste food colouring

200 g (7 oz) bar plain dark or milk chocolate

150 g (5 oz) white ready-to-roll icing

2 yellow and black liquorice sweets

Tips

• The butter icing could alternatively be
coloured and flavoured with about 4
teaspoons cocoa powder dissolved in
1 tablespoon boiling water instead of
using the food colouring, if preferred.

• If you are very short of time, use pieces
of chocolate flake for the lion's mane
and ready-coloured ready-to-roll icing.

1 Trim the top of the large round cake level, if needed. Put the
cake on to a chopping board and lay the mini sponge roll
on top in the centre for the lion's nose. Make 2 inverted 'V'
cuts, each about 5 cm (2 inches) deep and 5 cm (2 inches)
apart, beneath the nose to make the lion's jaw. Reserve the
trimmings for the ears. Round the jaw with a small knife, then
round the cheeks on either side.

2 Transfer the cake to the cake board or plate. Stick the ears in
place with a little butter icing.

3 Reserve 1 teaspoon of the butter icing. Colour the remainder
orange using a little each of the yellow and red colourings,
then spread all over the top and side of the cake.

4 Turn the chocolate bar over so that the smooth side is
uppermost. Run a swivel-bladed vegetable peeler over the
smooth side to make curls (see page 32). Press the chocolate
curls around the top edge of the cake for the lion's mane
using the flat edge of a round-bladed knife.

5 Knead and roll 2 small balls of white icing, flatten and shape
into thin ovals, then press on to the face for eyes. Add the
sweets for eyeballs, sticking them in place with a little of the
reserved butter icing.

6 Colour two-thirds of the remaining white icing deep orange,
shape into a curled tongue and press in place. Colour the
remaining icing black, shape into 2 flat rounds, then press on
to the base of the nose. Add small indentations with the end
of a cocktail stick. Store in a cool place until ready to serve.

Dancing dolphins

serves 10
decoration time 1 hour

Large round Quick-mix Sandwich Cake
  (see page 14)

double quantity Butter Icing (see page 21)

25 cm (10 inch) round cake board or plate

375 g (12 oz) white ready-to-roll icing

sifted icing sugar, for dusting

ice blue paste food colouring

250 g (8 oz) dark blue ready-to-roll icing

1 metre (39 inches) x 4 cm (1½ inch) wide blue
  chiffon ribbon

Tip
Instead of dolphins, why not try modelling
a boat with a fisherman or a sailor
onboard out of ready-to-roll icing?

1 Sandwich the cakes together with a little butter icing, then spread butter icing thinly around the side. Put on to the cake board or plate.

2 Knead the white icing on a surface lightly dusted with icing sugar until slightly softened. Knead in a little blue colouring until a pale even blue, then mix in a little more colouring until marbled with blue streaks.

3 Shape the icing into a long rope, then flatten with a rolling pin and trim to a strip 65 x 10 cm (26 x 4 inches). Press around the side of the cake, pressing the extra width over the top edge of the cake. Trim off any excess from the join.

4 Partially mix a little blue colouring into the remaining butter icing until it becomes marbled. Reserve 1 tablespoon of the icing, then swirl the remainder over the top of the cake to resemble the sea.

5 Knead the dark blue icing until softened slightly. Shape into 2 dolphins about 12.5 cm (5 inches) long by making a thick sausage shape and squeezing a nose at one end and a tapering tail at the other. Next, shape a dolphin head about 6 cm (2½ inches) long. Shape the remaining icing into small fins. Stick on to the dolphins with a little water or dots of butter icing. Make eyes by pressing a cocktail stick into the icing.

6 Arrange the dolphins on the cake, propping them up on pieces of pale blue icing so they look as if they are jumping. Spread the reserved butter icing around the icing support to resemble lapping waves. Tie the ribbon in a pretty bow around the cake.

Seasonal treats

Valentine cup cakes

makes 12
decoration time 30 minutes

single quantity Butter Icing (see page 21)

pink paste food colouring

12 Fairy Cakes (see page 16) or bought fairy
    cakes, with silver foil paper cases

200 g (7 oz) red ready-to-roll icing

sifted icing sugar, for dusting

10 chocolate sticks

75 g (3 oz) pale pink ready-to-roll icing

large round or square plate

1 Colour the butter icing pale pink with a little of the colouring. Level the tops of the cakes, if needed. Spread the tops of the cakes with an equal quantity of the butter icing.

2 Knead the red icing on a surface lightly dusted with icing sugar until slightly softened. Roll out and cut out twelve 5 cm (2 inch) hearts with a biscuit cutter, re-kneading and rolling out the trimmings as necessary.

3 Press the heart shapes on to 10 of the cakes. Cut the remaining 2 hearts in half with a zigzag line to symbolize a broken heart. Separate the halves slightly, then press on to the 2 remaining cakes.

4 For Cupid's arrows, break each chocolate stick in half, press one half into the centre of each unbroken heart and the other half as if coming out of the edge of the cake. Knead and roll out the pink ready-to-roll icing, cut out triangular arrow tips and 'V'-shaped feathers and stick on to the chocolate sticks with a little water or with tiny dots of butter icing from the scrapings in the bowl. Arrange on the plate and sprinkle the plate with heart-shaped foil graffiti, if liked.

Tip
Instead of adding the Cupid's arrows, pipe
on boys' and girls' names with tubes of
coloured writing icing.

Easter bunnies

makes 12
decoration time 30 minutes

12 Fairy Cakes (see page 16) or bought
   fairy cakes

single quantity Butter Icing (see page 21)

12 large white marshmallows

4 large pink marshmallows

12 mini white marshmallows

24 blue mini candy-covered chocolate drops

12 small square pink sweets

2 tablespoons Royal Icing (see page 25),
   coloured red, or 1 tube red fine
   writing icing

25 g (1 oz) pale pink ready-to-roll icing

sifted icing sugar, for dusting

large round or square plate

1 Level the tops of the cakes, if needed. Spread the tops of the
cakes with an equal amount of the butter icing.

2 Cut the large white marshmallows in half. With the cut side
uppermost, squeeze the corners to form into ear shapes.
Press 2 on to each cake, cut side uppermost. Cut the pink
marshmallows in half, then each half into slices. Press a slice
on top of each ear.

3 Cut the mini white marshmallows in half and press the cut
sides downwards on to the rabbit faces for cheeks. Add blue
candy-covered chocolate drops for eyes and square pink
sweets for noses. Pipe a mouth on to each rabbit with red
royal or writing icing.

4 Knead the pale pink icing on a surface lightly dusted with
icing sugar until slightly softened. Roll out and cut tiny strips
for whiskers. Press on to the rabbits. Arrange on a plate and
store in a cool place until ready to serve.

Tip

To save time on a party day, the cakes
may be made in advance, spread with the
butter icing and then frozen. Add the facial
features once the cakes have defrosted.

Ghostly ghoul

serves 10
decoration time 30 minutes

1 Put the cake on to a chopping board and cut into a long oval face shape. Curve the sides slightly to indicate hollow cheeks and a jaw. Cut the cake horizontally in half and sandwich back together with some of the butter icing. Spread the remaining butter icing thinly over the top and sides of the cake.

2 Cut off 200 g (7 oz) of the white icing, wrap the remainder and reserve. Knead on a surface lightly dusted with icing sugar until slightly softened. Add a little black colouring and knead until partially mixed and marbled. Roll out the icing thinly, drape over the cake board and smooth with your fingertips dusted with icing sugar. Trim off the excess.

3 Lift the cake on to the board. Pull off small pieces of the reserved white icing and shape into sausage shapes. Press on to the cake for eyebrows, lips, nose and frown lines. Roll out the remaining white icing and drape over the cake to cover completely, smoothing over the raised areas with your fingertips dusted with icing sugar. Trim off the excess.

4 Colour the trimmings black. Roll out a small ball of icing and cut a heart-shaped nose. Divide the remaining icing into thirds and shape each third into a small sausage. Flatten and shape into eyes and a mouth. Press on to the cake, sticking in place with a little water.

30 x 23 x 5 cm (12 x 9 x 2 inch) roasting tin
Medium Madeira Cake (see page 13)

double quantity Butter Icing (see page 21)

625 g (1¼ lb) white ready-to-roll icing

sifted icing sugar, for dusting

black paste food colouring

30 x 25 cm (12 x 10 inch) oval cake board

Tip

You may find it easier to dust the cake board with a little icing sugar and roll the marbled icing straight on to the board with a rolling pin.

spooky spiders

makes 12
decoration time 1 hour

12 Fairy Cakes (see page 16) or bought
   fairy cakes, with silver foil paper cases

single quantity Butter Icing (see page 21)

500 g (1 lb) purple ready-to-roll icing

sifted icing sugar, for dusting

18 black liquorice Catherine wheels

12 chocolate-covered marshmallow teacakes

24 pink candy-covered chocolate drops

24 mini blue candy-covered chocolate drops

1 tube black writing icing

large round or square plate

125 g (4 oz) pink or dark blue ready-to-roll
   icing

1 Level the tops of the cakes, if needed. Spread the top of each cake with a little butter icing. Knead the purple icing on a surface lightly dusted with icing sugar until slightly softened. Roll out and stamp out twelve 6 cm (2½ inch) rounds with a plain biscuit cutter. Press one on top of each cake. Re-knead and roll out the trimmings. Stamp out twelve 3.5 cm (1½ inch) plain rounds and press one on to each cake for a head.

2 Add a little butter icing to the centre of each cake. Unroll the liquorice and cut into 10 cm (4 inch) lengths. Add to each cake for legs. Cover the ends on each body with a teacake.

3 Stick 2 of the larger pink candy-covered chocolate drops on to each head for eyes with a little butter icing. Add the mini blue candy-covered chocolate drops for eyeballs and pipe black vertical lines down the centre with writing icing and tiny V-shaped nostrils.

4 Transfer the spiders to a plate and add small balls of pink or blue icing to the ends of the liquorice legs for feet.

Tip

For children who do not like liquorice, snip coloured jelly strips, such as those used for the grid in the Noughts and Crosses cake on page 60, into legs instead.

Jack-o-lantern

serves 8
decoration time 30 minutes

20 cm (8 inch) mixing bowl Small Madeira
   Cake (see page 12)

double quantity Butter Icing (see page 21)

yellow and red or orange paste food
   colourings

23 cm (9 inch) thin round cake board or
   large plate

50 g (2 oz) black ready-to-roll icing

sifted icing sugar, for dusting

125 g (4 oz) green ready-to-roll icing

1 Colour the butter icing orange with a little each of the yellow and red or orange colourings. Cut the cake horizontally in half and sandwich back together with some of the butter icing. Transfer the cake to the cake board or plate.

2 Spread a little butter icing thinly all over the cake to stick the crumbs in place, then spread thickly with more butter icing and smooth in downward lines with the back of a knife.

3 Knead the black icing on a surface lightly dusted with icing sugar until slightly softened. Roll out and cut out a large smiling mouth. Cut out small squares or triangles for missing teeth. Press on to the cake. Cut out triangles for eyes and a nose and press in place on the cake.

4 Knead and roll out the green icing. Cut out leaves of different sizes, mark on veins with a small knife then arrange on the cake top, curling and folding them slightly. Re-knead and roll out the trimmings. Cut long thin strips and curl these in and around the leaves to resemble tendrils.

Tip
Add the colouring little by little; you will find that you need less paste colouring than when colouring ready-to-roll icing.

Playful polar bears

serves 20
decoration time 1 hour, plus drying

23 cm (9 inch) deep round Large Madeira
    Cake (see page 13)

one-and-a-half quantity Butter Icing
    (see page 21)

28 cm (11 inch) thin round cake board or plate

750 g (1½ lb) pale blue ready-to-roll icing

sifted icing sugar, for dusting

single quantity Royal Icing (see page 25)

3 tablespoons desiccated coconut

250 g (8 oz) white ready-to-roll icing

black writing icing or an edible black icing pen

Tip

This cake could also be made into a
teddy's tea party by covering the cake in
pale green ready-to-roll icing, colouring
the royal icing pink and spreading it into
a smaller table-cloth shape. Add yellow
bears and a dolls' house tea service with
tiny plates and cups.

1 Trim the top of the cake level, if needed. Cut the cake
horizontally in half and sandwich back together with butter
icing. Put it on the cake board or plate and spread the
remaining butter icing over the top and side of the cake.

2 Knead the blue icing on a surface lightly dusted with icing
sugar until slightly softened. Roll out and use to cover the top
and side of the cake. Smooth in place with your fingertips
dusted with icing sugar. Trim off the excess.

3 Spoon the royal icing over the top of the cake and spread it
so that it dribbles over the sides. Ease into icicle-like shapes
with the point of a knife. Spread a little icing in patches on
the board or plate and up the side of the cake. Sprinkle with
the coconut, letting some fall on to the cake board or plate.

4 Knead the white ready-to-roll icing until slightly softened.
Shape 5 different-sized ovals of icing for the polar bear
bodies. Shape 5 round heads and make a small pinch in
each for a muzzle. Press the heads on to the bodies. Arrange
on the cake, sitting, lying or stretching up the side of the
cake. For the standing bear, you may need to attach the
body to the side of the cake with some royal icing scrapings
from the bowl. Shape sausage-like arms and legs, making
them slightly thicker where they join on to the body. To make
the ears, roll tiny balls of icing, then flatten and press on to
the heads, sticking in place with a little water. Roll any
remaining trimmings into snowballs of various sizes.

5 Leave the bears to harden, then pipe or write on face details
with black writing icing or an icing pen.

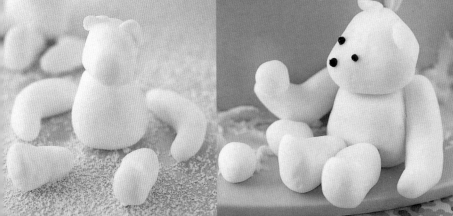

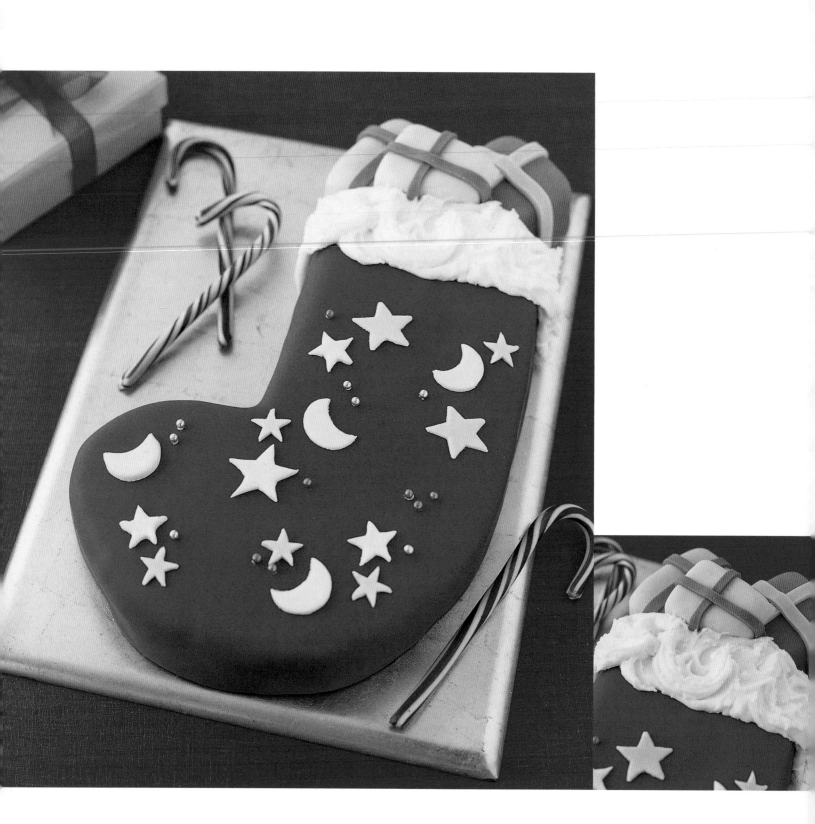

Christmas stocking

serves 10
decoration time 1 hour

1 Put the cake on to a chopping board and cut into a stocking shape about 11 cm (4½ inches) wide at the top of the leg. Cut 3 different-sized gifts from the trimmings and set aside. Cut the cake horizontally in half and sandwich back together with some butter icing. Spread a little butter icing very thinly over the top and sides of the cake and over the gifts. Transfer the stocking cake to the cake board or plate.

2 Knead the deep blue icing on a surface lightly dusted with icing sugar until slightly softened. Roll out and drape over the whole of the cake and smooth in place with your fingertips dusted with icing sugar. Trim off the excess.

3 Spread most of the royal icing over the top of the stocking and down both sides, then rough it up so that it resembles fleecy lining. Spoon the remaining icing into a greaseproof paper piping bag and snip off the tip (see page 31).

4 Knead and roll out the white icing and cut out rounds using a small round biscuit cutter, then cut partway into the rounds to make crescent moons. Cut star shapes with different-sized cutters. Stick the shapes on to the stocking with piped dots of royal icing. Repeat with a little pale pink icing. Add extra dots of piped icing and stick on rainbow pearls or silver balls.

5 Knead and roll out the deep pink, pale blue and remaining pale pink icings and cover one gift in each colour. Cut ribbons from the trimmings and stick on to the gifts with royal icing. Position at the top of the stocking. Add the candy canes to the cake board or plate.

30 x 23 x 5 cm (12 x 9 x 2 inch) roasting tin Medium Madeira Cake (see page 13)

double quantity Butter Icing (see page 21)

36 x 25 cm (14 x 10 inch) rectangular cake board or plate

375 g (12 oz) deep blue ready-to-roll icing

sifted icing sugar, for dusting

half quantity Royal Icing (see page 25)

75 g (3 oz) white ready-to-roll icing

75 g (3 oz) pale pink ready-to-roll icing

few rainbow pearls or edible silver balls

65 g (2½ oz) deep pink ready-to-roll icing

50 g (2 oz) pale blue ready-to-roll icing

selection of candy canes

Tip
If using a cake board, you may like to cover it with pale pink ready-to-roll icing before adding the cake.

Smiling snowman

serves 12
decoration time 1 hour

2 x 900 ml (1½ pint) pudding basin Medium
   Madeira Cakes (see page 13)

single quantity vanilla-flavoured Butter Icing
   (see page 21)

2 tablespoons apricot jam

15 cm (6 inch) thin round cake board or plate

1 Muffin (see page 17) or bought large muffin,
   paper case removed

triple quantity Royal icing (see page 25)

15 g (½ oz) black ready-to-roll icing

sifted icing sugar, for dusting

25 g (1 oz) orange ready-to-roll icing

50 g (2 oz) red ready-to-roll icing

25 g (1 oz) yellow ready-to-roll icing

Tip

The snowman can alternatively be
sandwiched together and covered with a
double quantity of vanilla or lemon butter
icing (see page 21) instead of royal icing.

1   Level the basin cake tops, if necessary, and sandwich the
trimmed tops together with the butter icing to make the
snowman's body. Spread jam thinly all over the outside of
the cakes to stick the crumbs in place. Stand the cake upright
on the cake board or plate. Press the muffin on to the body
so that the domed part of the muffin forms the snowman's
face. Spread the muffin with the remaining jam.

2   Spoon the royal icing over the cakes to cover completely,
spreading it as you go with a round-bladed knife and pulling
it into peaks with the back of the knife. Be careful not to
smear the jam into the icing.

3   Knead the black icing on a surface lightly dusted with icing
sugar until slightly softened and shape black eyes and 'coal'
buttons. Press on to the snowman. Knead the orange icing
and shape a tiny piece for the snowman's 'carrot' nose.
Press on to the snowman's face.

4   Knead the red icing, shape a tiny rope mouth and add to
the face. Shape half the remaining red icing into a round
and press on to the snowman's head for a hat.

5   Knead the yellow icing and shape into a rope 18 cm
(7 inches) long. Repeat with the remaining orange and red
icing. Twist the 3 colours together, then roll out to flatten.
Trim to a 36 x 2.5 cm (14 x 1 inch) strip. Make small cuts
in either end for a fringe, then wrap around the snowman as
a scarf. Re-knead and roll out the trimmings, fringe one side,
then roll up and add to the top of the hat for a bobble.

Index